Learn SAP® UI5

Copyright © 2015 by UI5CN

All rights reserved. No part of this publication may be reproduced, distributed, or transmitted in any form or by any means, including photocopying, recording, or other electronic or mechanical methods, without the prior written permission of the publisher, except in the case of brief quotations embodied in critical reviews and certain other noncommercial uses permitted by copyright law. For permission requests, write to the publisher, addressed "Attention: Permissions Coordinator," at the address below.

Rua Aquilino Ribeiro L280,

Pontinha, Lisbon

1675-292 PT

+351-968621883

www.UI5CN.com

1. The main category of the book — COMPUTERS > Enterprise Applications > General

TECHNOLOGY & ENGINEERING.

2. Another subject category — COMPUTERS > Web > Web Services & APIs

First Edition

Learn SAP® UI5

Learn SAP® UI5

Free Gift Coupons

Or
Go here

Learn SAP® UI5

Contents

1. INTRODUCTION 6
      1.1 Prerequisites 6
2. SAP UI5 Basics..7
      UI5 Libraries 7
      Explorer Section..7
      Setting of the Libraries...8
      Searching for Components...8
      UI5 Vs FIORI...9

Five UX key principles 10
      1.   Simple 10
      2.   Role Based 11
      3.   Instant Value and Delightful..12
      4.   Coherent...13
      5.   Responsive 14
      Setting up the development environment..14
      Procedure to prepare development environment 15
      Optional Tools..15
      Hello World Application..16

3. Use of Wireframe and Control Flow in App..20
      Create a Simple App 20
      Simple App Creation 21
4. Control Flow in UI5 App 24
      Instantiating your view controller 25
      Validating the control flow 26
      Extending the Application 28
      Model View Controller (MVC) 29
      Implementation in Eclipse 31
5. Popular UI5 Components and Data Binding..35
      Simple form creation...35
6. Data in UI5 Application 39
7. List 44
8. Table..48
      Table using:sap.ui.commons...49
9. Tiles...52
      Create Tiles Using Data Binding (JSON Data variable)...53

4

Learn SAP® UI5

10. Data Binding Using Factory Functions 56
    NAMED MODEL 57

11. Using Chrome Development Toolkit 59
    Elements tab 60
    Toggle Device Mode 62
    BROWSER CONSOLE 62
    Source..63
    Network...64
    Responsiveness and Browser Compatibility 64

12. Styling and Theming for UI5 App 65
    Styling and Theming, advance options 68
    Media Query 68
    THEME DESIGNER 68

13. Using Events and Handling Events 72
    EVENTS 72
    Events in Real Project 73
    Events in Tables 76
    Advance Events..77
    Capturing and Bubbling 79

14. Miscellaneous Controls in UI5 83
    UX3 Control – SHELL 83

Fragments...85
    Split Screen Application 87

15. App Improvement Elements 90
    FORMATTER 90
    Internationalization and Localization...91

16. Data Visualization Using UI5 94
    Viz : Bar Chart 94
    Viz : Pie Chart..96
    KPI Tiles 98

Referencing and Bibliography 101

Learn SAP® UI5

1. INTRODUCTION

The SAPUI5 is a platform for developing rich user interfaces for modern Web business applications. It is supported by the browsers that support HTML5 capabilities in a web application. An application built with SAPUI5 is responsive across browsers and devices - they run on smart phones, tablets, and desktops (device that supports HTML5). The responsiveness is provided by the UI controls, which automatically adapt based device type.

1.1 Prerequisites

The skill sets you need to start with UI5 are HTML5, CSS3, JavaScript, jQuery and OData. Even if you don't know any one of these skill set, it is not difficult to learn it over a period of time as most of the technologies are easy to learn.

Below is an image that shows how much one need to be efficient in these technologies to start working with UI5.

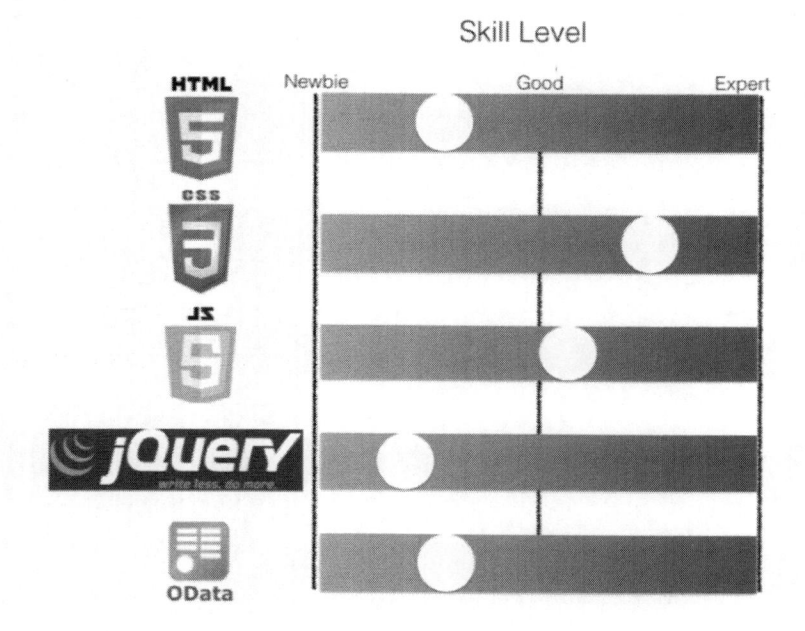

You can also check our SAPUI5 Professional Development video course for accelerated learning: here or use the below QR code.

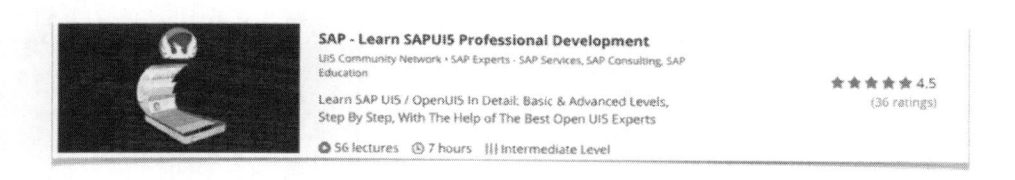

6

Learn SAP® UI5

2. SAP UI5 Basics

Let's start with the UI5 libraries. If you want to work in an enterpriseproject using 'SAPUI5', then you have to understand the 'UI5 Libraries' very well.

UI5 Libraries

Before starting with SAP UI5 development, you need to understand the UI5 libraries so you know 'How to use them' and 'When to use them'. There are two different UI5 libraries present in the marketplace:

    Open UI5 (with Apache 2 License)

    SAPUI5 (with SAP License)

The OpenUI5 is free and you will be allowed to use it without any permission from SAP. However, to use SAPUI5 you need to have an existing SAP license.

The current version of Open UI5 library is "Version 1.36.6" (The versions change frequently. Due to many numbers of developers involved in improving the libraries.)

Explorer Section

The Explorer section is where you can see all the components and know how the individual components will behave, when we use those components in application.

    Let's look at the libraries at https://openui5.hana.ondemand.com/explored.html

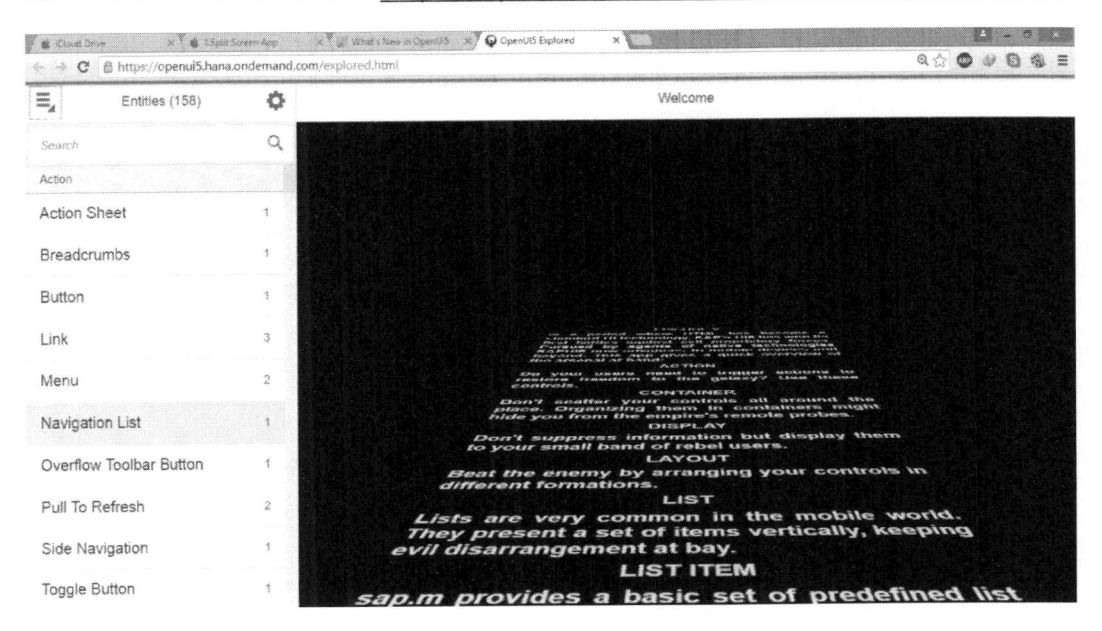

Learn SAP® UI5

Here we have a master detail layout where in the left side we have list of components and in the right hand side detailed description of the components and how it will behave when you are using those components in your application. In mobile devices, it automatically adapts and shows the master detail layout in the same screen for better User Experience.

Setting of the Libraries

When you click on the settings icon on your left hand side of the screen, you will get settings to change for which theme you want to see the components. Here we have two main themes available. *Blue Crystal Theme* and *High contrast black*.

Searching for Components

It also contains a search option to search for specific component that you can use for UI5 Application. For Example: If you want to add a list item in your application then you will search for 'list' keyword to get the filtered results that containing the keyword "list".

Here let's select the simple list by clicking on it, you will get the detailed information about the list, like which library it belongs to (here it belongs to "sap.m" this is present from 1.10 Version of SAP UI5). We can see lot of examples here, these all are individual examples showing how to use this list item on different type of scenarios.

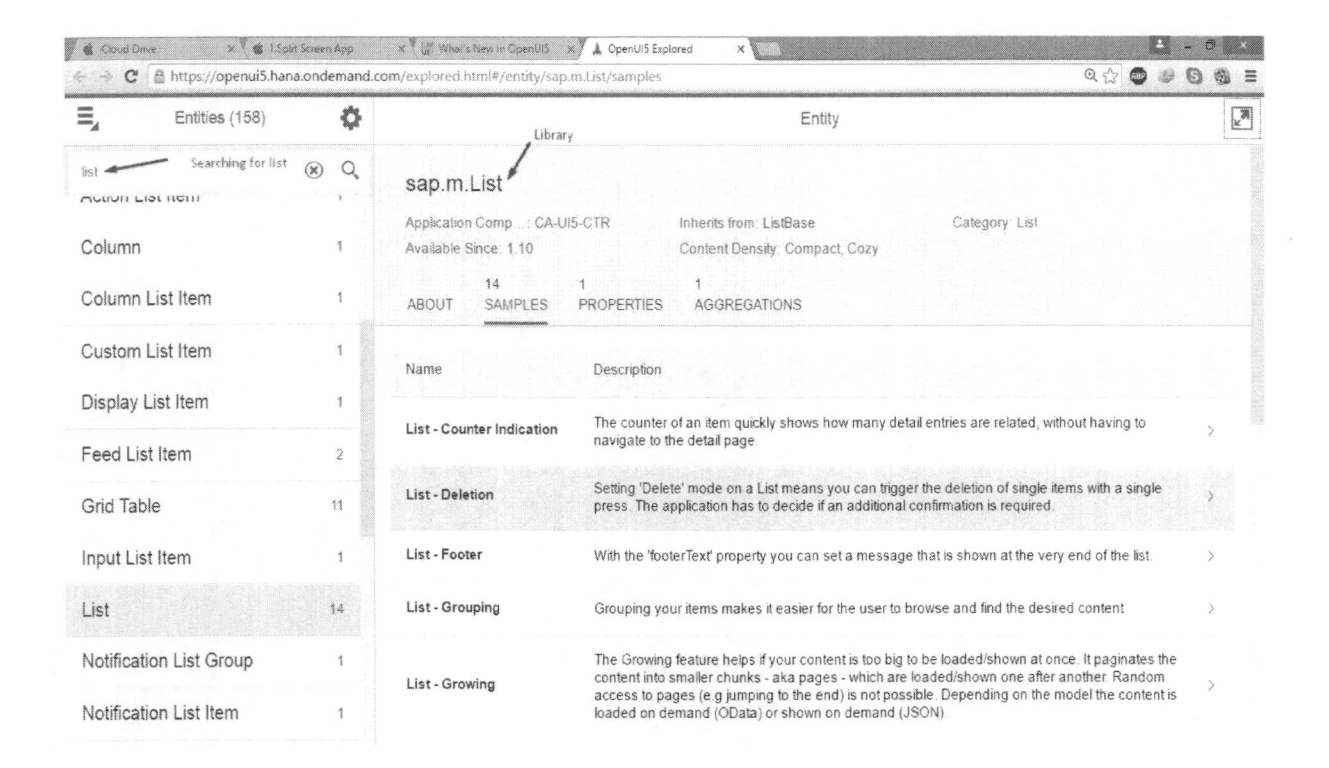

8

Let us look for the first one "List-Counter Indication". Click on that and you will get the description and the number in the right hand side (here it is number of products in that Power Projector 4713 category).

If you want to see the code click the icon, you have on the right hand corner as shown below:

On pressing that, you can see we have two files. XML File and Java Script File. These two files are responsible for generating the content that we see after we clicked the "List-Counter Indication". This helps a lot in the process of development when you are looking to add some components and you want to get a quick access to the code. You can also see the behavior of the code by clicking back.

At the detailed description page, you have these details like Samples, About, Properties and Aggregations. The Properties and Aggregations will be required at the time of development like, the properties the component have and what type of aggregations. These are frequently used in your project. We will discuss it briefly in the components section in this course.

UI5 Vs FIORI

One of the popular names, which you might hear, is Fiori. Many of you might have this have this question what is FIORI? And how it is related to UI5? So let us consider the Lego blocks for explain this. If UI5 is Lego blocks then FIORI is the finished product. SAP FIORI are the pre-build applications which SAP ships and SAP UI5 are the building blocks to create these applications. Here main importance is given to User Experience (UX). Basically there are five rules which one has to follow to create these applications. These five rules are followed in all the FIORI applications and if you are going to build any application for the purpose of consumption then you should follow these five key principles.

SAP UI5 is the building box   FIORI is the finished application using SAPUI5

Learn SAP® UI5

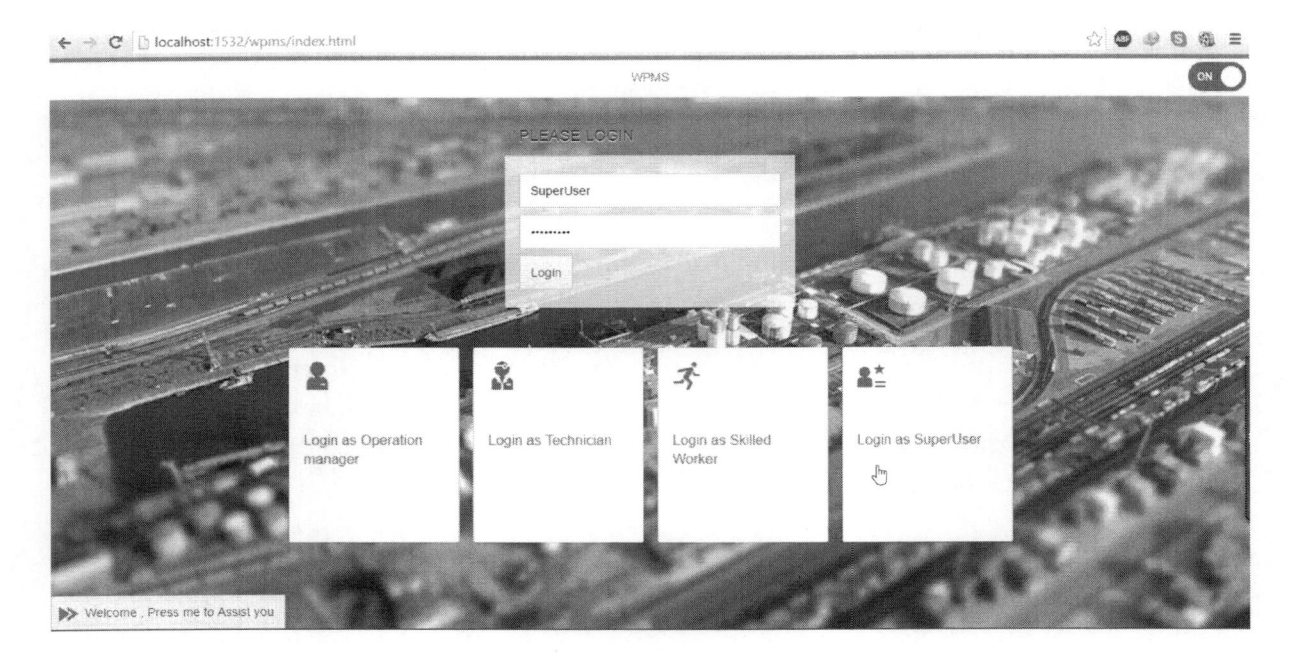

Five UX key principles

Now we will look into these 5 key principles with an application called WPMS (Work Permit Management Solutions). So let see how these five key principles mapped out to an UI5 Applications.

This is the sample application, which was created for demonstration purpose for this book. The application is built with UI5. We are going to see how these five user experience principles are used while creating this application.

1. Simple

This is the home screen and it is quite simple. It has a user ID, password and a login button. We also have an Assist button on the left hand corner of the screen. When you press the assist button, you will get tiles. When you press any of the tiles then the input fields are automatically filled up. So you can log in with these credentials. Once you do that, you can see another tile screen where you have a lot of functionalities and features.

If we logged in as a Super User then we have total seven tiles. And each belongs to one business functionality.

This will be an underlying principle thought out the application where you will notice that navigation, use of applications is simple, and users can work on this application without any user-manual.

Learn SAP® UI5

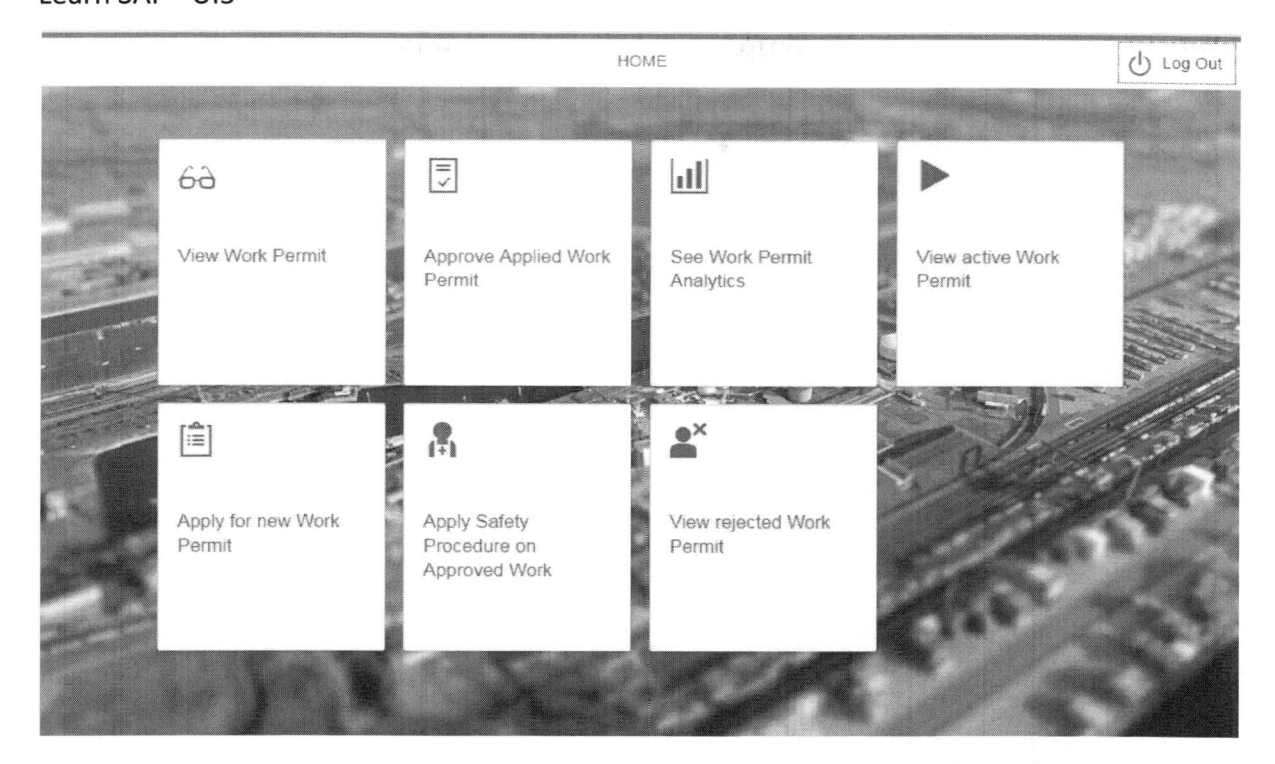

Home Screen for Super user with all functionalities, which are **simple** to use.

2. Role Based

If we, log out from Super User and come back to the home screen. And again login as "Technician". Here you will get only see five functionalities, which are provided for technician. This is the second principle "The Application should be Role-Based". If you login as a Super User you have more functionality and if you login as a Technician, you are allowed to see only five functionalities. This is depending upon business Process. Depending upon your role the functionality will be changing.

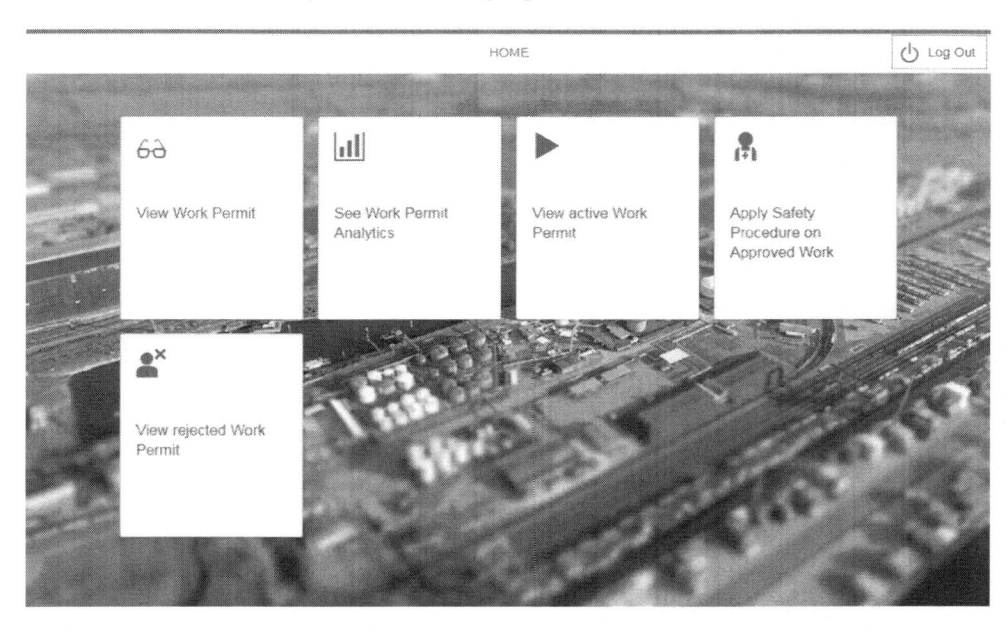

Home screen for Technician with only 5 functionalities, so the app is **role-based**.

Learn SAP® UI5

3. Instant Value and Delightful

Let us login with the super user again and select the "View work permits" to see all the work permits with the status on the right side. You can also filter the work permits depending upon the status. Simply search it on the 'filter status box' on the right hand side.

If you want to see all the approved work permits, you simply type *"approve"* on the box then you will get all the approved work permits on the screen. You can also check the details of the work order number by clicking on it.

Another way to filter the content is using the work order number. You have to type the work order number on the left hand side then you will get the work permits filtered out.

Searching for work permits by typing few words of the status to filter permit by status.

See Work permit analytics:

If you want to have an overview idea about the status of work permits, then you can go into analytics section and you can see an analytic chart. Here you can see the status of work permits corresponding to the work orders. The status bar is mentioned in different colors according to the status like Applied, Active, Approved, De-active and Rejected. It is easy to see the work order has number of work permits and status in an Analytic visualization. It gives us an instant and delightful experience.

Learn SAP® UI5

We can see the third work order "200710135" has multiple work permits like two of them are already active, one is approved, one is deactivated and one is rejected.

4. Coherent

The application should be coherence. For example: If Operational manager is going inside the application to activate a work permit then the user interface of that is almost similar to view work permit. This will give user a similar user experience and create no chance for confusion while using the application.

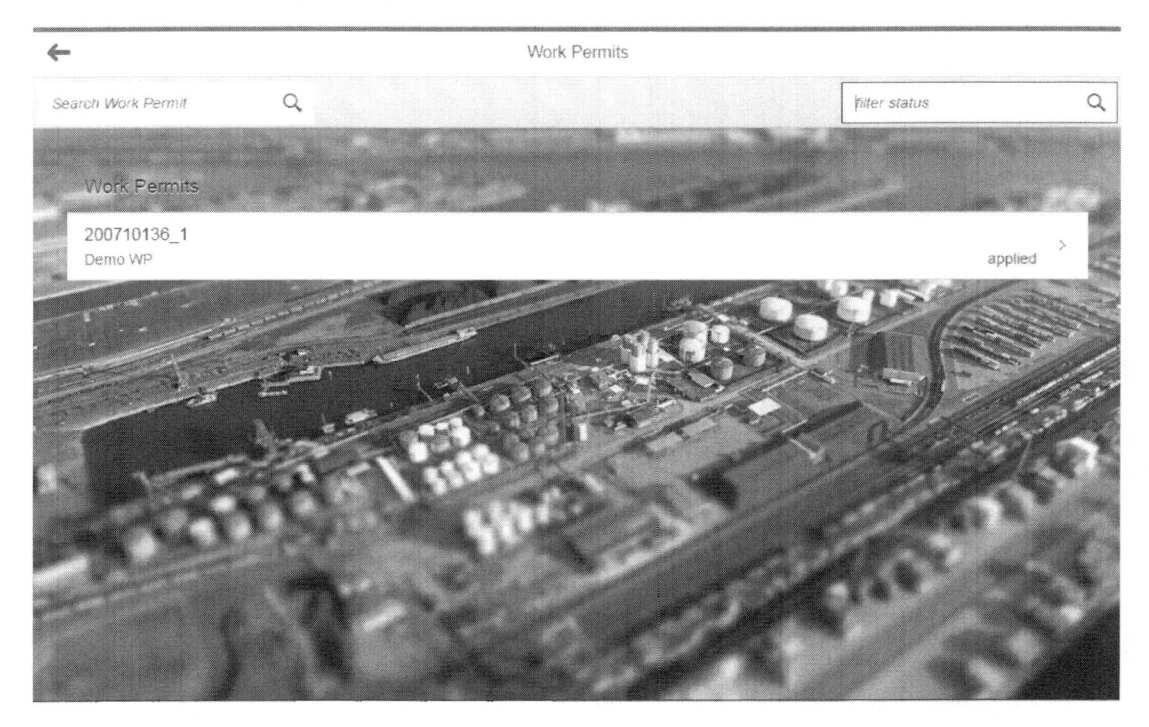

Learn SAP® UI5

5. Responsive

The last key principle is Responsive. We already know the application can support all the devices. Therefore, it should be responsive in all the devices like computers, tablets and Smart phones. We should be able to use all the features like work permits, filter option, analytics, etc. in all these devices.

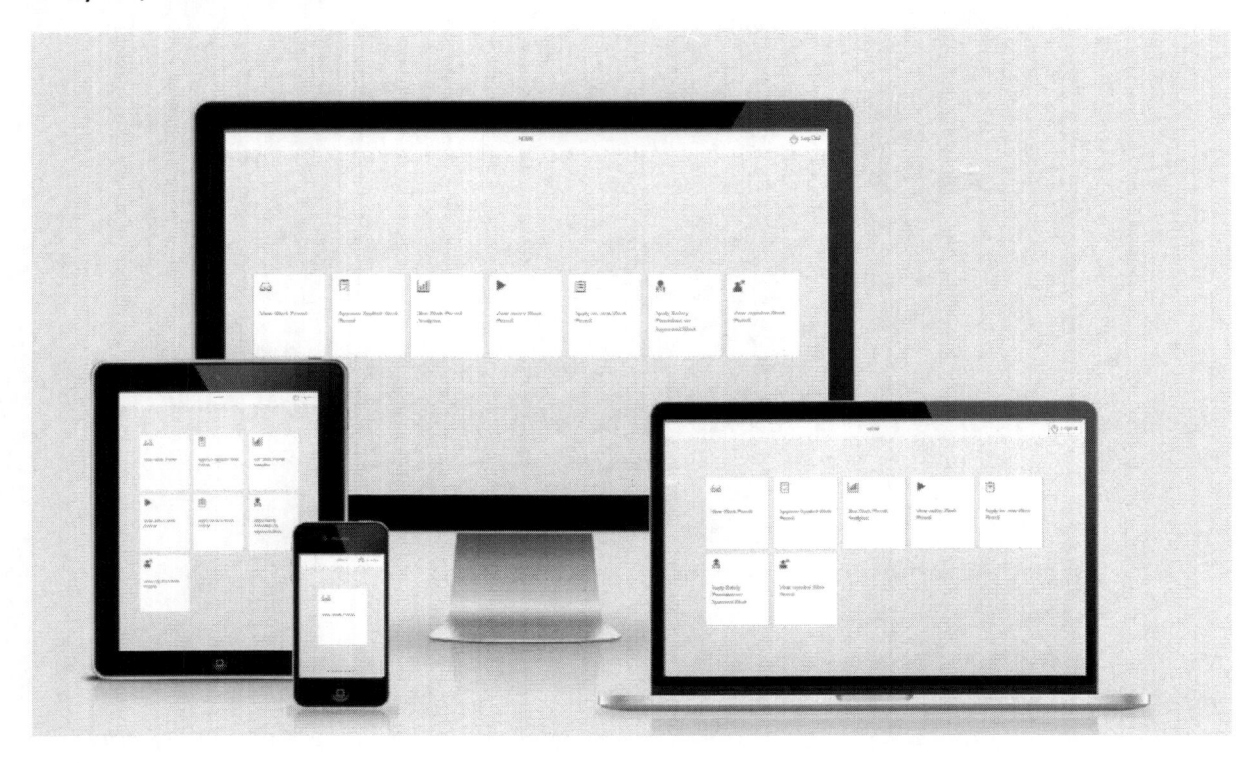

Setting up the development environment

To setting up the development environment, we need to download the "Eclipse lunar" and we are going to add the UI5 repositories to it.

Eclipse Luna IDE: Eclipse is used to do your complete project and editing with this IDE. https://eclipse.org/downloads/.

Go to this link and you will directly land in the download page. It automatically detects the Operating system. In Windows there are two versions available 32 bit and 64 bit. To check this right click on "My computer or This PC" in your desktop and select properties, then find your system type. You need to download depending upon your system type.

Java: Java will be required to run Eclipse and you can download it from:

https://java.com/en/download/

After installing eclipse repository, you need to install UI5 components below are the steps which archives that or you can also go to https://tools.hana.ondemand.com/#sapui5:

Learn SAP® UI5

Procedure to prepare development environment

1. After installing eclipse open it and go to help. You can see install new software, click on it you will get a new window. As we are using eclipse Luna we should use https://tools.hana.ondemand.com/luna to get repository content, paste this URL into the box. Once you pasted the URL, you will be able to see all the components, which can be installed in your eclipse.

2. We are focusing on UI5. So select the UI5 development toolkit for HTML5 from that list. You can additionally select other tools, but adding unrequited tools will affect the performance of the IDE. After selecting your UI Components, click next.

3. In the next page it may show the versions which will be added to eclipse. Click Next. You have to accept the license agreement and click Next to Finish. Once you finish these steps, your repository content will be installed. And the progress of installations steps depends upon your speed of internet connection.

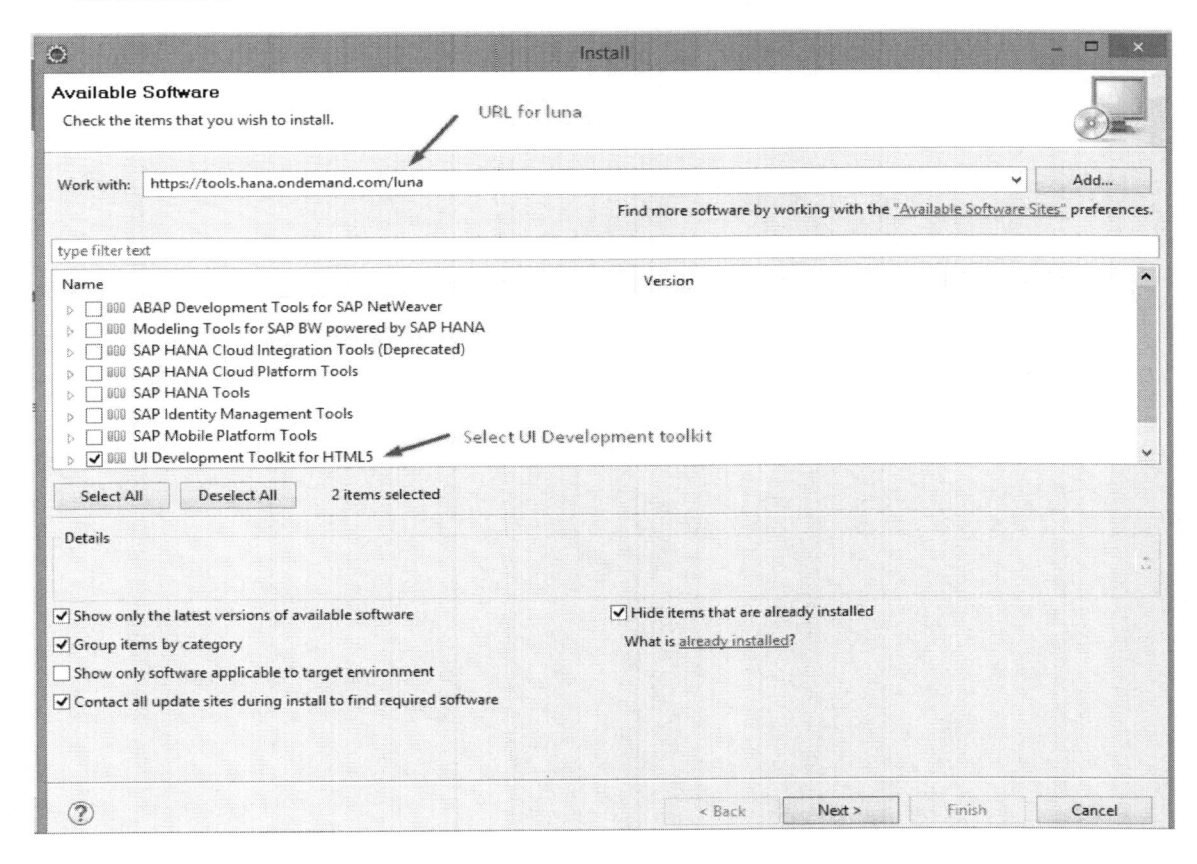

Optional Tools

Sublime editor (Optional): Sublime editor is similar to other editors like Notepad++. The sublime editor has lot of features to search, to replace and editing purpose. If is fast, free and small. www.sublimetext.com

Learn SAP® UI5

Cloud9 IDE: It is a cloud based IDE which is used to write your code, compile and access it anywhere. You need to create an account to use the Cloud9 IDE and it is free. We will be sharing a lot of codes in Cloud 9 IDE and are going to use it for lot of development. One of the major benefit of using cloud based IDE is that the entire development environment are Pre-Packed and in coming future most of the development are going to be done based on Cloud environment, so getting familiar with Cloud9 will be a major boost. Link for Cloud9 IDE https://c9.io/

All demo files are available in the repository. It will be useful for your development of the project as well, when you need access to quick syntax. It is made public and you can access it and see live preview of the code in URL :https://ide.c9.io/ajaytech/demo

Hello World Application

Let start with the coding using UI5 Application. It will be a hello world application. If you already worked with an UI5 Application, you can simply skip this step because it will be very basic Hello World Application.

To create a new project Click File -> New -> Other. You can see the SAP UI5 Development. If you cannot find the SAP UI5, you can search it using keyword UI5. It will filter down the results. Now select the application project on the screen and click next.

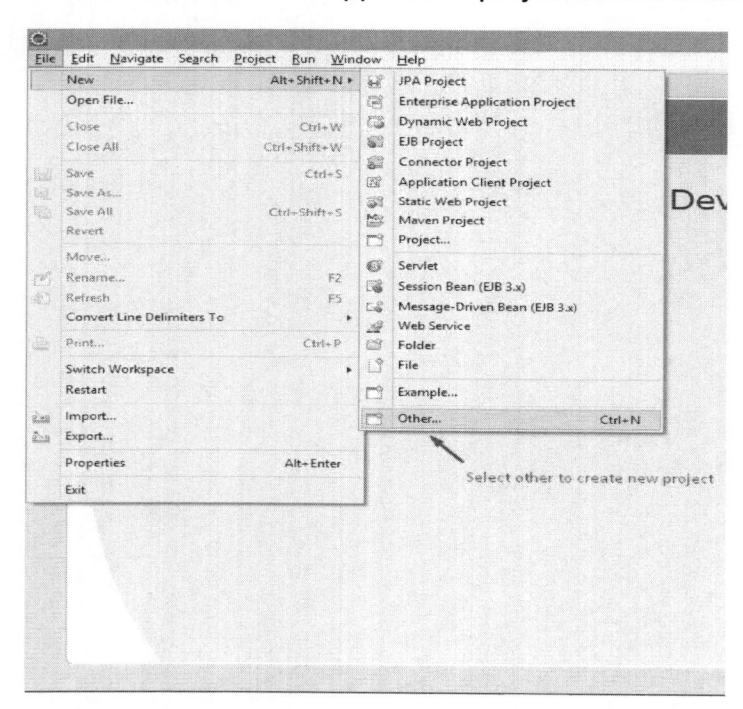

You will be asked to enter your project name. Choose your own project name. Let us select myFirstApp_01 for our first project name. The location of the project will be saved at the workspace folder by default, which is the location where eclipse artifacts are present if you have not changed the workspace manually.

Learn SAP® UI5

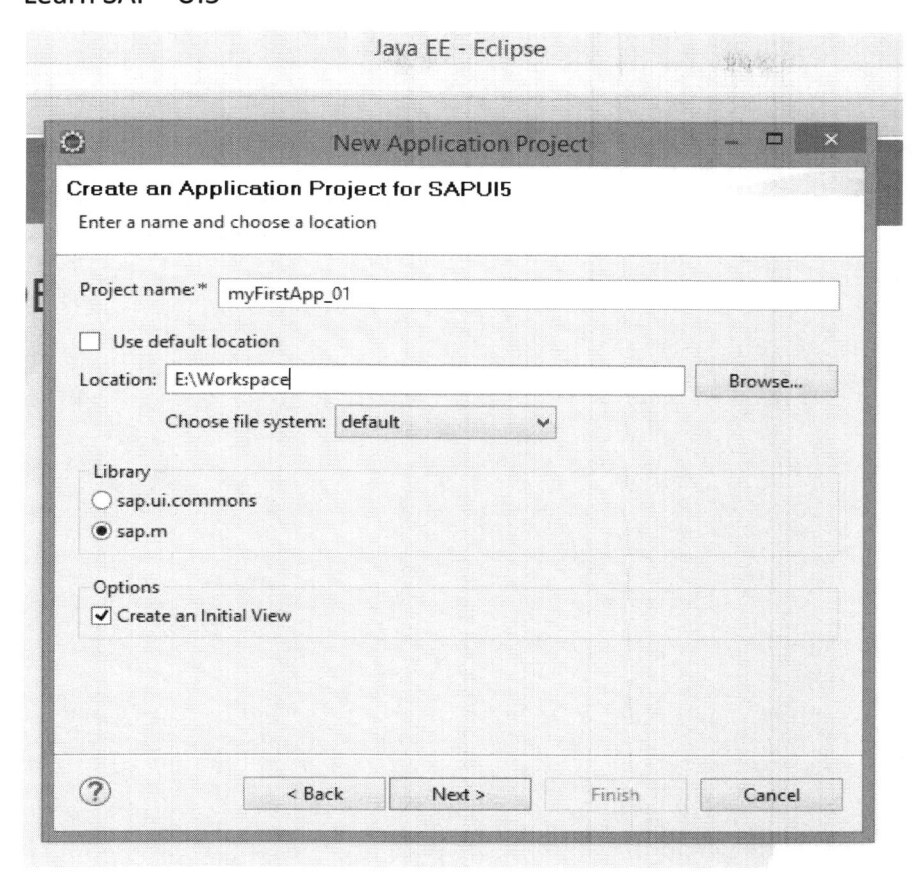

[Screenshot: New Application Project dialog in Java EE - Eclipse. "Create an Application Project for SAPUI5 - Enter a name and choose a location". Project name: myFirstApp_01. Use default location unchecked. Location: E:\Workspace. Choose file system: default. Library options: sap.ui.commons, sap.m (selected). Options: Create an Initial View (checked). Buttons: Back, Next, Finish, Cancel.]

Below are the options, which you need to select, to start your first project:

- **Library**: Here there are two libraries sap.ui.commons and sap.m library. And we are going to use the sap.m
- **Options**: It is having a checkbox option. If you need the initial view to be created by default, then keep the checked option and click next.

In this page, we have to give a name to your view controller pair. Here we have given *demo* as the name.

In the next page, you must have a list to select which type of view you need. You have the options like JavaScript, XML, JSON and HTML. The JavaScript and XML are common in UI5 Application but most people find JavaScript is easier to work with. When you are building an enterprise application, then there is a highly likely chance that you will require a lot of customization, which are not out of box. So using JavaScript is ideal for getting extra flexibility.

On final screen, it will show all the libraries that will be added to the application now click finish. It will create your Application.

Now you are all set to start development in your first application. You can see three tabs *index.html, demo.controller.js, demo.view.js*. It is inside a folder called *myFirstApp_01*. This is the same name of the project, which we provided in project creation wizard.

Learn SAP® UI5

The index.html file is the centre of action and is the location from where program execution begins. We run this file to start our application. To start with, let us go to demo.view.js and change tile of the page to 'Hello World' instead of 'Title'

Code for demo.view.js :

```
sap.ui.jsview("myFirstApp_01.demo", {

    /**SpecifiestheControllerbelongingtothisView.
     *Inthecasethatitisnotimplemented,orthat"null"isreturned,thisViewdoesnothaveaController.
     *@memberOfmyFirstApp_01.demo
     */
    getControllerName : function() {
        return" myFirstApp_01.demo";
    },

    /**IsinitiallycalledonceaftertheControllerhasbeeninstantiated.ItistheplacewheretheUIisconstructed.
     *SincetheControllerisgiventothismethod,itseventhandlerscanbeattachedrightaway.
     *@memberOfmyFirstApp_01.demo
     */
    createContent : function(oController) {
        returnnew sap.m.Page({
            title: "Hello World",
            content: [

            ]
        });
    }

});
```

On running the code by right click on the index.html file from project explorer tab. There will be two major options provided 'run on server' and 'Web App Preview'. If you add some server to your eclipse like Tomcat then you can run the application on Tomcat. In the current application, we only have HTML5 and Java Script related artifacts so we can also go for Web App Preview. Once you press the Web App preview, you can see the result in the IDE. Congratulations! You have created your first Hello World Program.

You can also copy the URL and paste it in your web browser to see the result. We will be using chrome browser a lot in this course. It is very robust and complete development toolkit, which will be required for front end UI Developers.

Learn SAP® UI5

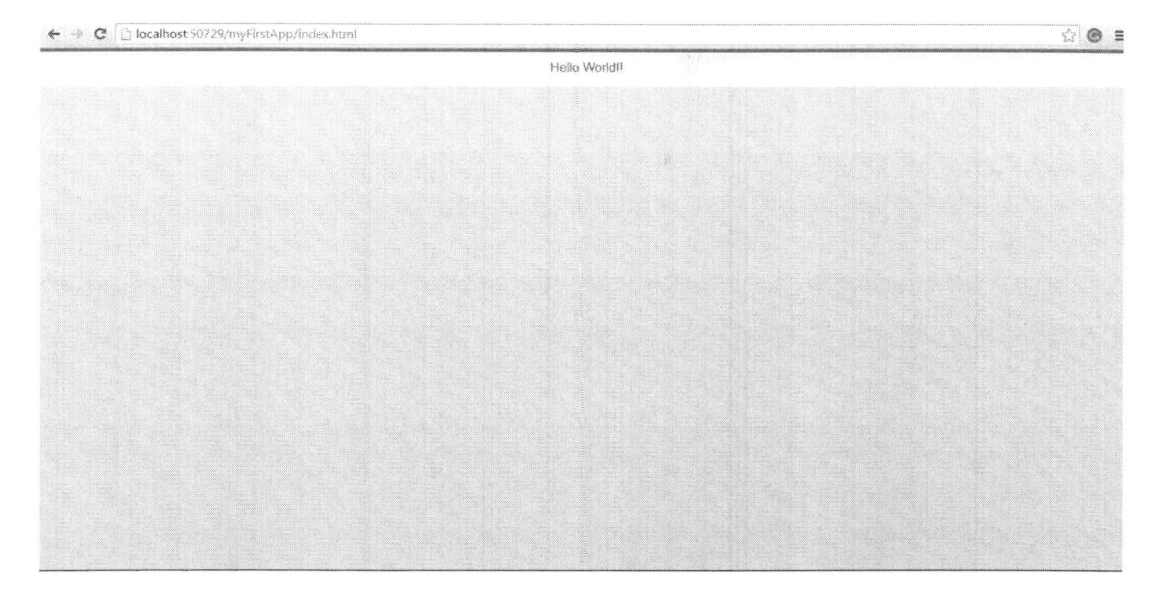

You can also check our SAPUI5 Professional Development video course for accelerated learning: here or use the below QR code.

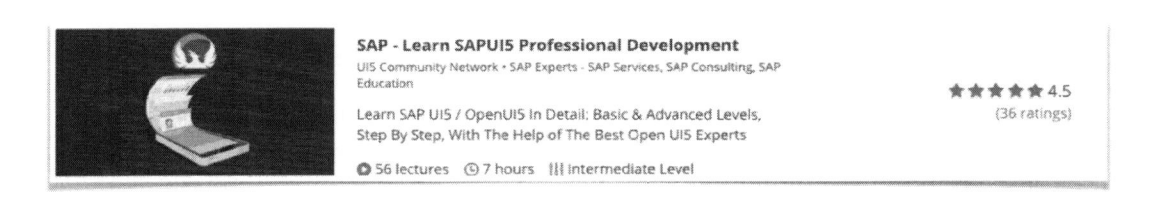

Learn SAP® UI5

3. Use of Wireframe and Control Flow in App

Create a Simple App

Now before going to the code walkthrough let us create a Simple App. To create a simple application we have to create a wireframe. Wireframes are used to bring clarity to your design. A mobile application or Website should go through a phase where all the requirements should be clear.

We are going to use moqups to create wireframes. Moqups(http://moqups.com) is an online tool to create wireframe. It is also a wonderful online wireframing tool, which can be used for free up to certain limit.

Once you visit www.moqups.com it will ask you to login. You can login using your Google account as well. After login, create a new page here. In this page, we can use any components, which are present in the left side of the design area.

For example if you want to use an input box just drag and drop it into the right hand side. It also has a mobile component you can search it under the components tool bar. We will drag and bring it to design area. Now if you want to place the input box on the mobile phone component right click on the box and select the 'bring it forward' option. This will place the input box on the mobile screen. Double click on the box and put a name. Here let us give it a label 'Enter Name'.

Let's create a simple App

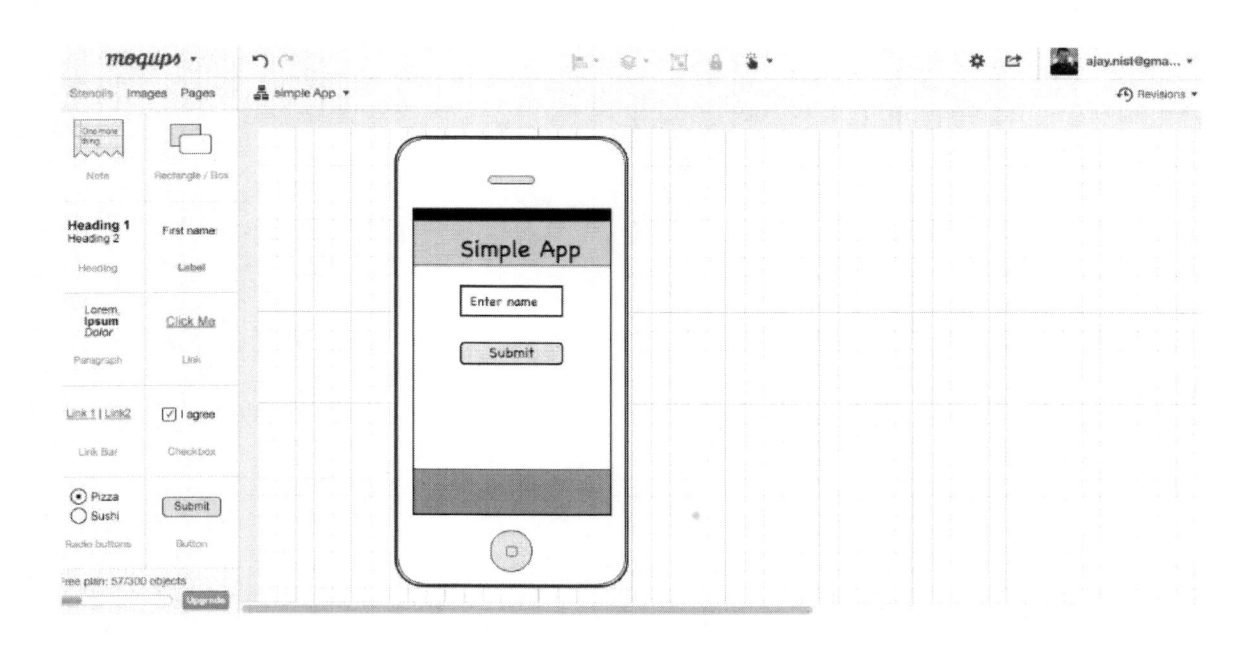

Learn SAP® UI5

For this simple application, we will use input box and a button. Let us add a button by search in the search bar under the components on left hand side. It will filter the button components. Select the button and drag it onto the mobile phone. Double click on it and name it as 'Submit'.

Now we need a label (labels are text content) for title of the page. Search for label on the components search bar and drag it to the mobile phone screen top. Change the name of the label as 'Simple App'. That is it. This is the mockup, which we are going to build in UI5. Finally, we have a simple application with a title as 'Simple App', an input box as 'Enter name' and a Submit Button. Let us go into the eclipse and start developing the application.

Simple App Creation

Now we are in eclipse. We are going to create a simple application. The first step was to change the heading. For this, we can go inside the view. Here you can see the code *sap.m.page* with the title property as "Hello World". Now we are going to change the hello world into 'Simple App' (Exactly what was mentioned in our wireframe).

If we refer back to our wireframe, we need to create one input box and one button now. For this, I have to go inside my Open UI5 library by following link

https://tools.hana.ondemand.com/.

In this case, we need the Explorer and API Reference. Open both in different tabs. We can search in the explorer for any application components or Elements, which we are going to use. We have to search for the 'Input' component that we require right now. Search it in the box provided on the left side tab. When we search it with sap.m.Input we will see a lot of result, we need to select JSDoc one for sap.m.Input . Here we should check first the version which will open in the version of UI5 library. As our eclipse version is 1.34 so we can use it in our project.

Next step will be to see how this looks in Explorer with an example. If we go to Explorer and search 'Input', we will see many results, select the first example 'Input – Assisted' and you can see the output how it will look. To view the source codes click the icon on the right top corner. This will be XML view, which we will get; here you can see what code will be used for input tags. For our purpose, we need an input with a placeholder ('Enter Name') and we can see in example that we need to use property 'text' for that. Let's go into our eclipse and use 'sap.m.input'.

Now we can go in view file in the eclipse and we are going to change the code according to our project.

```
createContent : function(oController) {
        var oSimpleInput = new sap.m.Input({
            placeholder:"Enter Name"
        })
        var oBtn = new sap.m.Button({
            text : 'Submit'
        })
        var oPage = new sap.m.Page({
```

```
                    title: "Title",
                    content: [
                        
                        oSimpleInput,
                        Btn
                    ]
            });
            return oPage;
        }

});
```

In this case, we can see that the variable name is oSimpleInput (It is always better to have the beginning of the variable with the meaning representing what kind of variable it is. We are creating an object for sap.m.Input. So here 'o' refers to Object value, if it would be an array then 'a', If it will be an integer then 'i' and so on). Therefore, oSimpleInput here is an object of sap.m.Input.

We need to pass the parameter 'place holder' (Better copy and paste the keywords. Because spelling mistakes in keywords are the most common errors). Inside the placeholder type 'Enter name' as per our wireframe.

We are also going to create a variable oPage and at the end of the function *createContent* and return it. We are also going to put oSimpleInput into the content of this page.

After adding input button, we go for the next component button. This will follow the same steps as we have done for Input. Search for the component button and select button component. We have to look for the source code by clicking the icon on the top right corner. Here I look for the properties of the button as required in our wireframe. We can also get details of the button using the API Reference (this we cover later). Go to eclipse and add the object button with its property as 'text' and save the file.

To run this file we do not need to follow the steps that we followed initially done. In addition, if you have already opened the web page, then click on 'Reload'. And the new result will be shown.

Let's try to run it in the Google chrome browser you will get the result. Here you can see the input text box is width is by default 100% of the page and the submit button on left hand side. These are some of the CSS properties and changes that we are going to see in later section.

Learn SAP® UI5

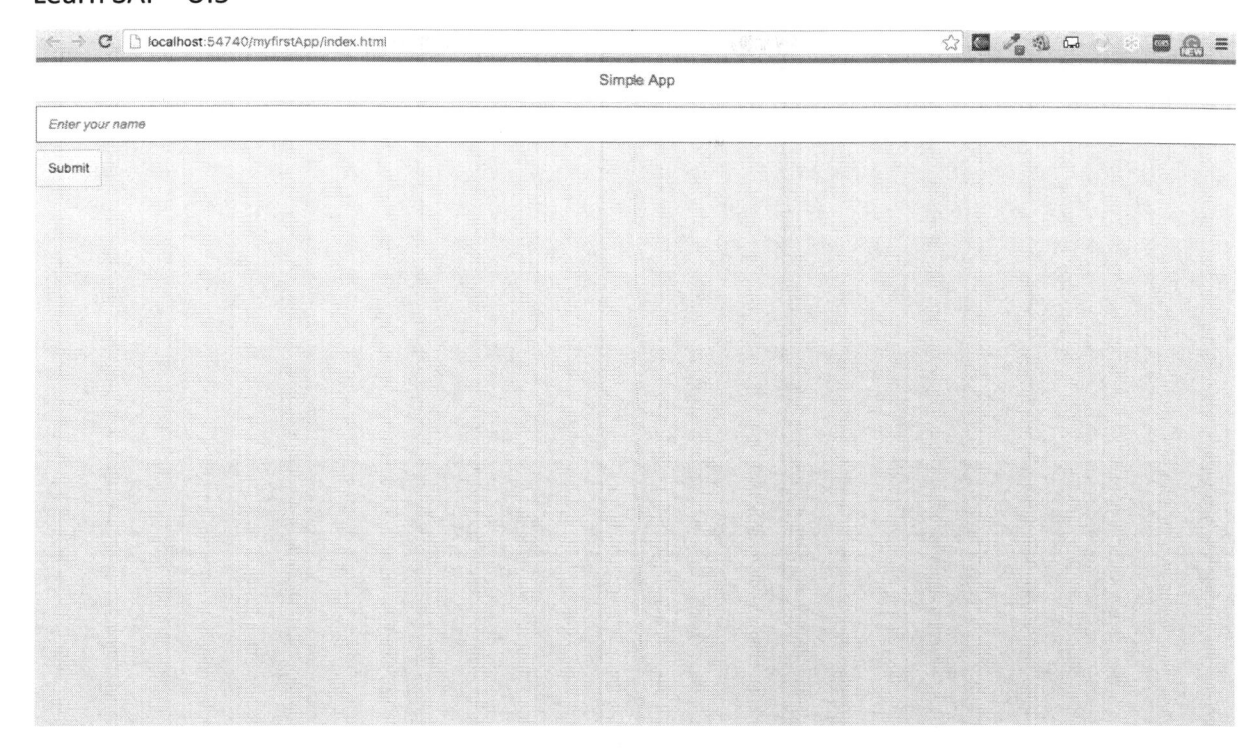

You can also check our SAPUI5 Professional Development video course for accelerated learning: here or use the below QR code.

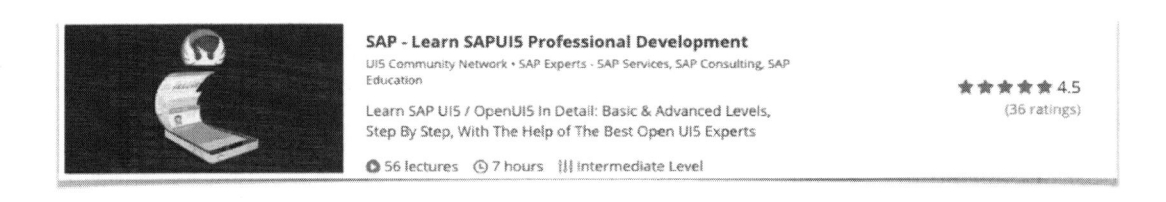

Learn SAP® UI5

4. Control Flow in UI5 App

If we look at the control flow in our UI5 Application the program execution starts from the index file which is 'index.html'. The first action is loading our library file.

```
<script>
src="resources/sap-ui-core.js
id="sap-ui-bootstrap"
data-sap-ui-libs="sap.m"
data-sap-ui-theme="sap_bluecrystal
</script>
```

You can see here the "src='resource/sap-ui-core.js'" will load the core library file for our UI5 Application. This process is also called as **Bootstrapping**. Here you can also mention the library file that is required for our application. One more thing we need is which are the libraries we require for our application in this case it is 'sap.m'. Here you can see that we are only mentioning 'sap.m' but sometimes we may require some feature, which needs analytics in your application. In that case we will use library called 'sap.m,sap.viz'. Which you will be mentioning beside 'sap.m'. Similarly, there is lot of other libraries like "sap.ui.commons". We will see these in future sections.

The theme, which we are going to use here, is blue crystal theme. It is the most commonly used theme in UI5 Application and also the default theme which is created when you create the project. In future, we will also see the process of creating own custom theme or using custom CSS.

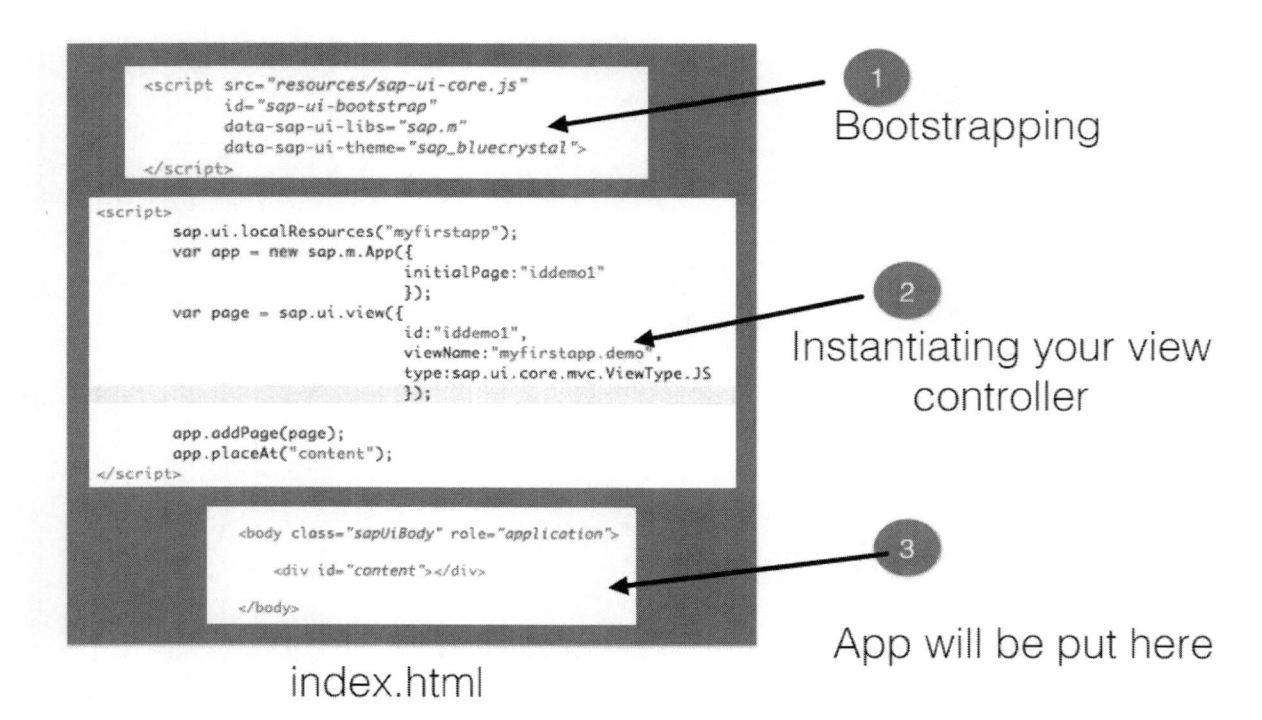

```
<script src="resources/sap-ui-core.js"
        id="sap-ui-bootstrap"
        data-sap-ui-libs="sap.m"
        data-sap-ui-theme="sap_bluecrystal">
</script>
```
1. Bootstrapping

```
<script>
    sap.ui.localResources("myfirstapp");
    var app = new sap.m.App({
                        initialPage:"iddemo1"
                        });
    var page = sap.ui.view({
                        id:"iddemo1",
                        viewName:"myfirstapp.demo",
                        type:sap.ui.core.mvc.ViewType.JS
                        });
    app.addPage(page);
    app.placeAt("content");
</script>
```
2. Instantiating your view controller

```
<body class="sapUiBody" role="application">
    <div id="content"></div>
</body>
```
3. App will be put here

index.html

Instantiating your view controller

2 Instantiating your view controller

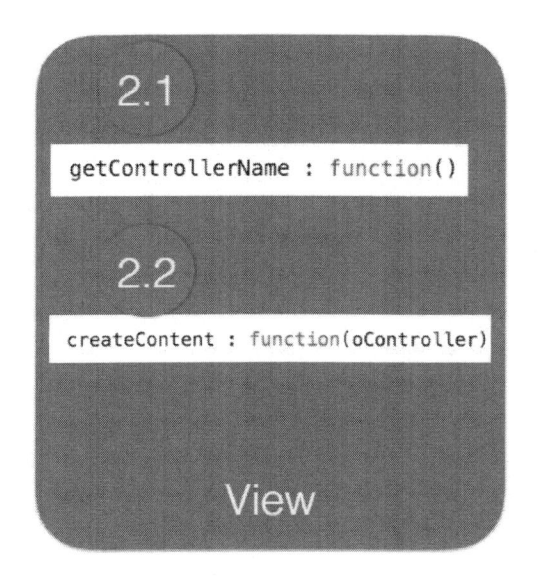

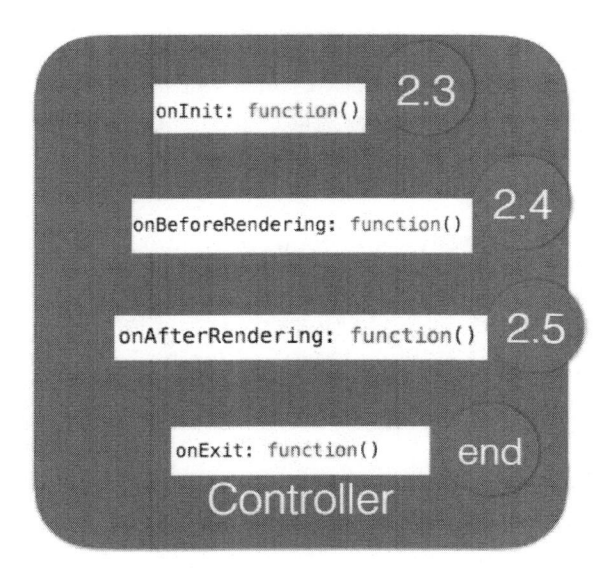

View (2.1, 2.2):
- 2.1 `getControllerName : function()`
- 2.2 `createContent : function(oController)`

Controller (2.3, 2.4, 2.5, end):
- 2.3 `onInit: function()`
- 2.4 `onBeforeRendering: function()`
- 2.5 `onAfterRendering: function()`
- end `onExit: function()`

The next step after bootstrapping is instantiation. Here you create object for your app, object of your view controller and you add the view into your app. Then you place the app at content.

```
<script>
    console.log("in index page creating app object");
    sap.ui.localResources("myfirstapp_01");
    var app = new sap.m.App({initialPage:"iddemo1"}); <!— Creating Object
                                                           for app —!>
        var page = sap.ui.view({id:"iddemo1", <!— Creating object of view
                                                  controller -!>
            viewName:"myfirstapp_01.demo",
            type:sap.ui.core.mvc.ViewType.JS});
    app.addPage(page); <!— Adding the view to the page -!>
    app.placeAt("content"); <!- Placing App at content -!>
</script>
```

You might be having one question regarding, what is content? content is actually the ID of the Div element mention in the index page (`<div id="content"></div>`). And your entire application will be placed inside it.

Instantiating your view controller

If we see the view and controller, they are always in a pair. You can have the view without the controller. However, those are special cases.

getControllerName

In the view, the first step is execution of *getControllerName*. Once the function in this view is executed, the program will come to know the name of the controller.

createContent

After getControllerName*createContent* function will be executed. At the end of the *createContent* function the page object will be returned. This is actually contains all the components like text box, input box which we mentioned in content section of the oPage.

onBeforeRendering

Before creating the content of the page there are two functions, which will be executed. First one is *onInit*. *onInit* function that is written in controller, which will be followed by the *onBeforeRendering* (Before the page is actually rendered. That is when the objects of all the elements are created).

onAfterRendering

After the *onBeforeRendering,*function*onAfterRendering* is executed and it will continue until we exit the application.

onExit

At the end function when you exit or close the application, onExit function is executed. This is the control flow of the application. Let's go into the eclipse and validate this control flow.

Validating the control flow

We are going to write the *console.log* inside each of our default function. *Console.log* is a common object/method provided by debuggers (including Chrome Debugger and Firefox debugger) that allows a script to log data into JavaScript console.

First, we write the console.log inside the script of index file.

```
<script>
    console.log("in index page creating app object");
            sap.ui.localResources("myfirstapp_01");
            var app = new sap.m.App({initialPage:"iddemo1"});
            var page = sap.ui.view({id:"iddemo1",
viewName:"myfirstapp_01.demo", type:sap.ui.core.mvc.ViewType.JS});
            app.addPage(page);
            app.placeAt("content");
</script>
```

Similarly add console.log inside the view file.

```
sap.ui.jsview("myfirstapp_01.demo", {

/**SpecifiestheControllerbelongingtothisView.
```

Learn SAP® UI5

```
       * In the case that it is not implemented, or that "null" is returned, this View doesn't have a Controller.
       * @memberOf myfirstapp_01.demo
       */
        getControllerName : function() {
            console.log("getControllerName");

            return "myfirstapp_01.demo";
        },
```

Write the console.log inside the controller file in *onInit*, *onBeforeRendering*, *onAfterRendering* functions as well.

```
sap.ui.controller("myfirstapp_01.demo", {

/**
* Called when a controller is instantiated and its View controls (if available) are already created.
* Can be used to modify the View before it is displayed, to bind event handlers and do other one-time initialization.
* @memberOf myfirstapp_01.demo
*/
        onInit: function() {

            console.log("onInit");

        },

/**
* Similar to onAfterRendering, but this hook is invoked before the controller's View is re-rendered
* (NOT before the first rendering! onInit() is used for that one!).
* @memberOf myfirstapp_01.demo
*/
onBeforeRendering: function() {
      console.log("onBeforeRendering");

        },

/**
* Called when the View has been rendered (so its HTML is part of the document). Post-rendering manipulations of the HTML could be done here.
* This hook is the same one that SAPUI5 controls get after being rendered.
* @memberOf myfirstapp_01.demo
*/
onAfterRendering: function() {
      console.log("onAfterRendering");

        },

/**
* Called when the Controller is destroyed. Use this one to free resources and finalize activities.
* @memberOf myfirstapp_01.demo
*/
        onExit: function() {
            console.log("onExit");
```

Learn SAP® UI5

```
    }
});
```

Save the project and reload it in the browser. Right click anywhere on the screen and select inspect element then a console will be opened.

Now we can see the control flow from our result in the console window based on the execution of our app. The sequence you will find is

1. Index page
2. getControllerName
3. createContent
4. onInit
5. onBeforeRendering
6. onAfterRendering.
7. onExit(if you close the application)

By this, we get a clear idea about how the control flow of an application works. It is essential when creating a big application that contains larger components involved to predict the outcome of the application.

Extending the Application

Let us extend our application and bring it to the next level by adding more components to it. We already had seen the Simple App example now we are going to extend it by adding a new view controller with back button and label on the second page. First, we are going to build a wireframe for this and then start the development process.

Before moving to that we want to clarify how to work with MVC pattern, it is one of the most common pattern in programming language and with UI5 it is a bit different in implementation.

Learn SAP® UI5

Model View Controller (MVC)

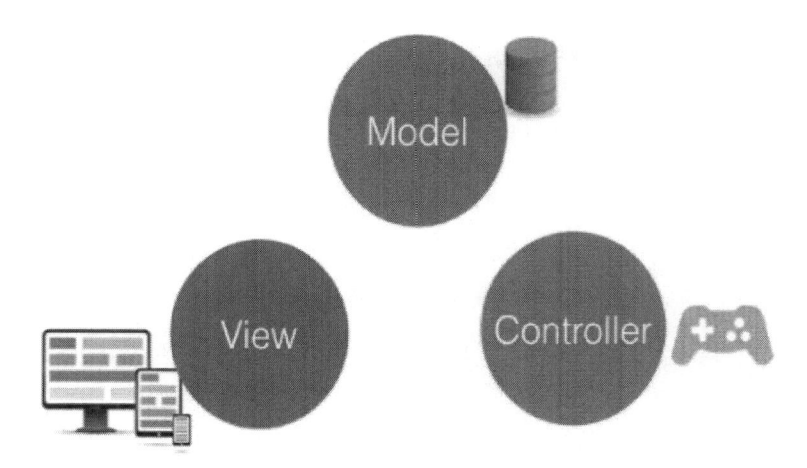

MVC Stands for **Model View Controller.**

View

The first step is to see what the requirement of view. It can be a wireframe or it can be design blue print or even a sketch drawing in pen and paper. For extending this application with extra elements, we need add a back button and label on the second page.

Controller

The second thing is what the functionalities these components will perform. For example, what will happen when we press the back/Navigation button or what action needs to be performed when click on a label?

In addition, if we enter some data in input field and hit enter, should it go to second page and display that data.

Model

Anything, which we input in the application or the application, is consuming it from some source. It can be from a database or a web service. These are the models, which is the data for the application. We should be aware about what are the data types which are involve in the application, how we are presented those using view controller. UI5 contains some nice set of libraries to do all these model operations. In the coming sections, we are going to see model related functions in detail. This is the MVC pattern. Let us build the wire frame and after building the wireframe, we will go to implementation of the design in Eclipse.

Learn SAP® UI5

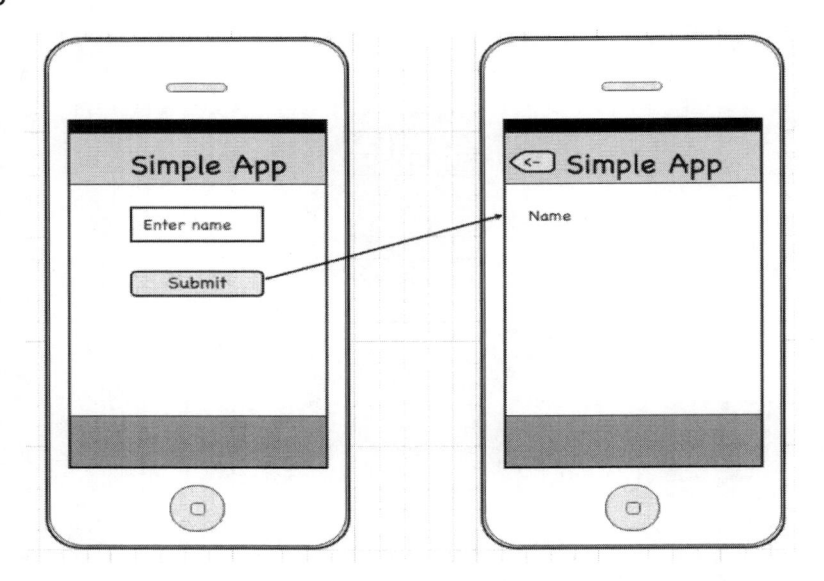

We already created a simple App. Now we are going to extend it. Here we have a wire frame using moqups. In this new design, we need a second page. It is similar to the first page so we can just copy and paste the entire mobile layout for the second page. Rename the simple app into 'second page', remove the Input and submit button, as we don't need that.

Now we are going to add a back button by selecting it from the components list. We can rename it to with back arrow '<-' instead of 'Back' text. In addition, we need to add a label so we can select the label from the components, place it on the screen, and rename it to 'Name'.

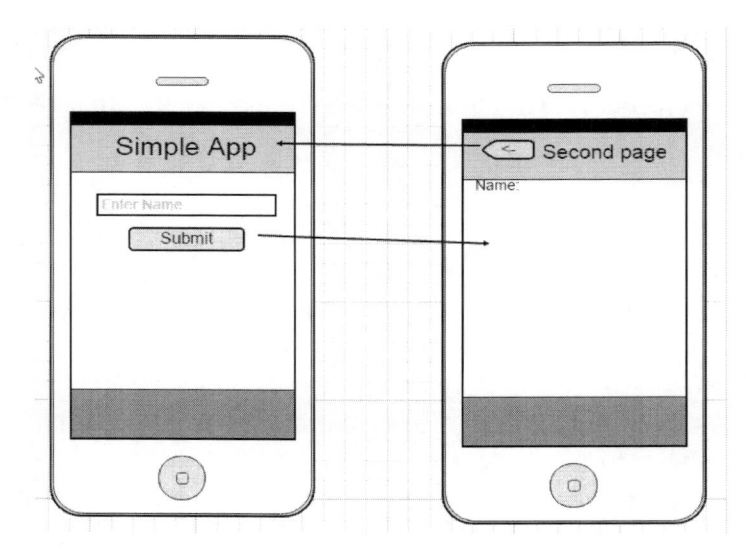

If you are working with multiple developers involved in your project, then you can add arrows to represent the events. For example if we click the back button on the second page, it goes to first page. Search it from the component list in moqups and select the appropriate arrows to represent an event. This will be more intuitive as the event is also represented in the diagram.

Learn SAP® UI5

Implementation in Eclipse

Once we finish the wireframe, we can go to eclipse and create a new project with the project name 'twoPageSimpleApp'. Select the library sap.m and check mark the 'create an initial view'. Click next and give the view name as 'first' then select JavaScript. Click finish then it will build the project for us.

Now it will open our first view. We have to change certain things in createContent function, which return an sap.m.Page object. Create an oPage object (Here in oPage the 'o' suggests the object. It is a camel code notation. Camel code is a practice of writing compound words or phrases such that each word or abbreviation begins with a capital letter. Example iPhone, eCommerce, bigfoot etc.) When you are using some variable in your application, it is always good to use a prefix, which signifies its type. It may be the integer type, string type or Boolean type. Here our oPage object starts with o signifies it is an object. Now we are going to return the oPage.

We can recreate the page that we already created in previous section. Here we need to add the input and button.

```
createContent : function(oController) {

    var oSimpleInput = new sap.m.Input("idInput",{
    placeholder: "Enter your name"
    });
     var oSimpleButton = new sap.m.Button("idButton",{
    text: "Submit",
    press:[oController.goToSecondPage,oController]

     /**Event listener to navigate to the second page after
     clicking submit */
    })

        var oPage = new sap.m.Page({
        title: "Simple App",
        content: [
                oSimpleInput,
                oSimpleButton

        ]
    });

    return oPage;            /** Return the oPage */

}
```

Controller function

In the controller we add the function 'goToSecondPage: function(oEvt)'. By adding this, controller will know what to do when the button is pressed.

Learn SAP® UI5

View controller for second page

We need to create a new View-Controller for second page. For this we go to New -> others,

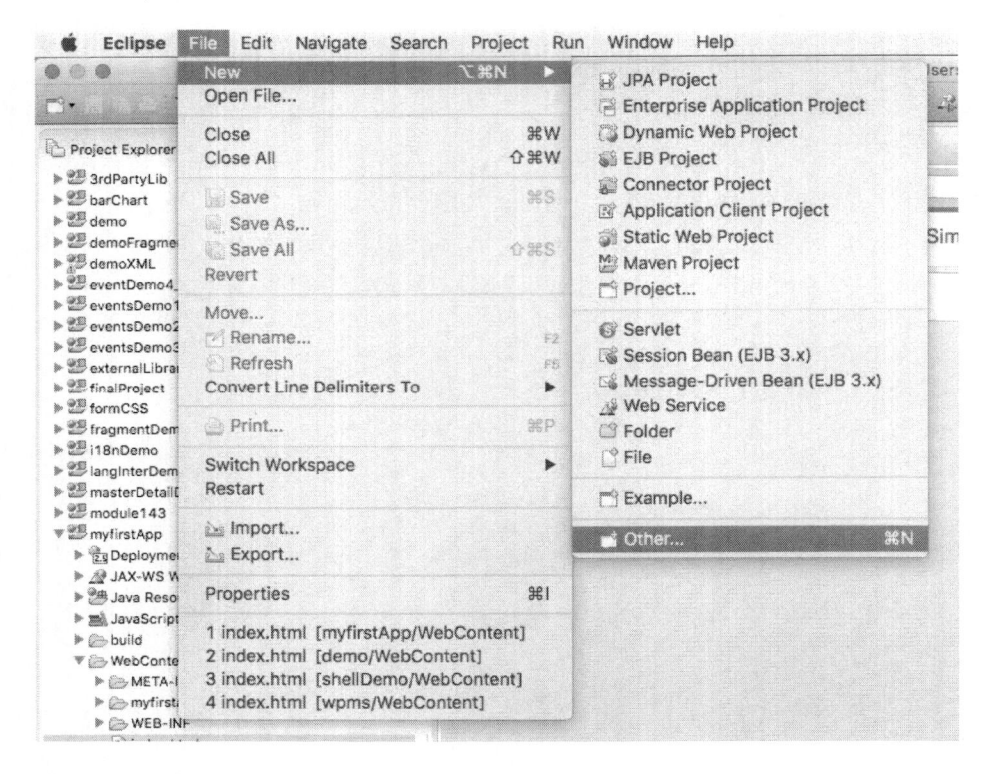

search for view, click next, and name it as 'second'.

This will create the second page. I am changing the page to oPage instead of returning the page itself. It is not compulsory but it gives more clarity to understand the code when, if it starts to become complex. Then we need to add a new label called 'oLabel' and assign it to sap.m.Label. In addition, we assign an ID to the label.

```
createContent : function(oController) {
    var oLabel = new sap.m.Label("idLabel"); /**Adding new label */

    var oPage = new sap.m.Page({
        title: "Second Page", /**Title for Second Page */

        showNavButton:true, /**It understands that we need a
                    navigation button */

        navButtonPress:function(oEvt){app.back();},/**Action Listener
            to perform action when navigation button is pressed */

        content: [
            oLabel
        ]
    });
    return oPage;
}
```

Learn SAP® UI5

Now we need to instantiate the second page. In the index file, we only have a single page created and by default when we create the application the code to instantiate, the page was added there. Here we can use the syntax for first page instantiation, which was automatically generated with the project and change the names as shown below:

```
var page1 = sap.ui.view({id:"idfirst1", viewName:"twopagesimpleapp.first",
type:sap.ui.core.mvc.ViewType.JS});/**Instantiation for first page */
var page2 = sap.ui.view({id:"idSecond1",
viewName:"twopagesimpleapp.second",
type:sap.ui.core.mvc.ViewType.JS});/**Instantiation for second page */

app.addPage(page1); /**Adding page 1 */

app.addPage(page2); /**Adding page 2 */
```

Now the page2 is available in the application but how can we navigate to the new page?

To achieve that we are going to use its id . And use the function `sap.ui.getCore().byId("idSecond1")` which will give the object of corresponding UI5 element.

```
goToSecondPage : function(oEvt){

    var oLabel = sap.ui.getCore().byId("idLabel");
    var oInputVal = sap.ui.getCore().byId("idInput").getValue();
    if(oInputVal !== undefined){
        oLabel.setText(oInputVal);

        /* Navigate to second page */

        app.to("idSecond1");
    }

},
```

Once we complete requirement. Run the application in chrome. Enter some text in the box and press the submit button. It is not going anywhere. Oh no! We have a bug.

So right click and inspect, open the console window and you can see what the error is. Here it is showing that 'oLabel.setValue' is not a function. To fix it, we are going to run the code in the console itself to verify the code, which was written, is correct or not. Go to the first.controller and copy

  '`var oLabel = sap.ui.getCore().byId("idLabel");`'

Paste in the console and hit enter. It is fine here. Let us check the oLabel has the function called 'setValue'. It is not here so check if 'setText' is present. Let's change the 'setValue' to 'setText'. This way of finding out if a function exist for an object is pretty common, some may call it hit and trail, but when you are going to work with UI5 it is going to be difficult to remember all the function and no one actually does that as well !

Learn SAP® UI5

Now run the application in chrome again. Yes, we get the exact result that we are expecting. Enter some text in the input and press submit. It goes to the second page, the text you entered is shown there in a label and we can navigate back to first page.

In coming section, we will see how to work with data and to add more components to your UI5 Application.

You can also check our SAPUI5 Professional Development video course for accelerated learning: here or use the below QR code.

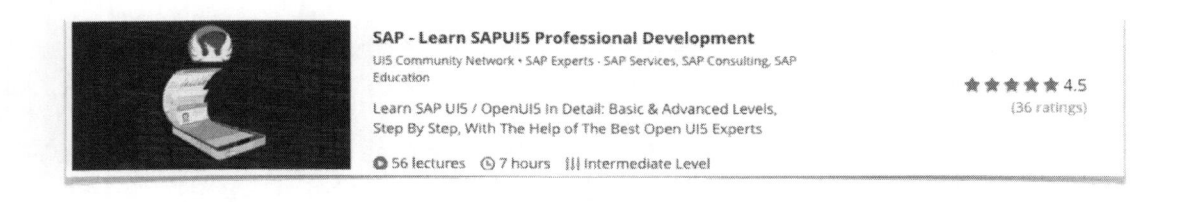

34

Learn SAP® UI5

5. Popular UI5 Components and Data Binding

Simple form creation

There are many components present in UI5 libraries and many of them are very frequently used in our project. In this section, we are going to see how to use some of the most common components. When you are using these components, you will be constantly looking into the API Reference and Explorer. In Explorer, you will find how the components will result and in the API reference, the syntax and details are available.

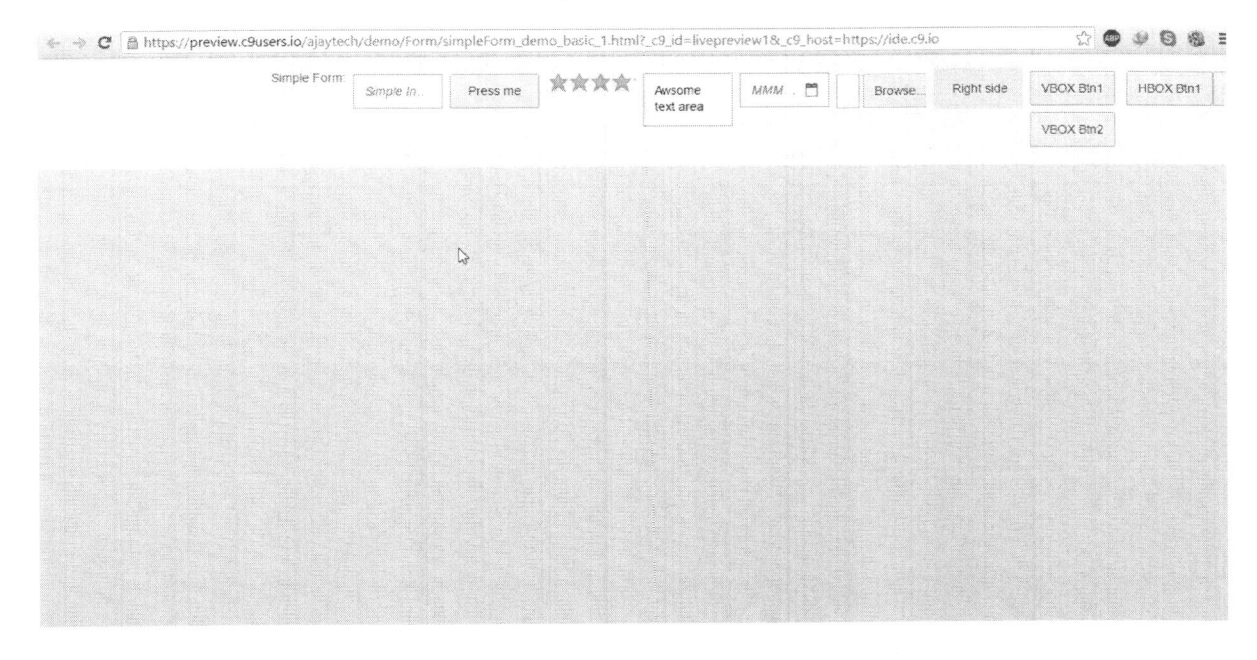

In the cloud9 IDE we already had the basic setup for creating our UI5 Application. The main reason to go with cloud 9 IDE is to create a demo, which can be accessible globally to reader.

The first thing we need is a simple form. For this go to explorer and search for simple form. Once you click on the simple form, you will get the library details like how to use this and which component it belong to. Copy the library and paste it in API reference and search. In the results, we are interested in JSDoc Report. Click on it and we will get more details about the function we can use and all the function/properties, which are borrowed, from its parent. We also have aggregation, which we will see in detail later. Now we work on the simple form and add it to our projects.

To add a simple form use 'var oSimpleForm = new sap.ui.layout.form.SimpleForm'. We need to pass few properties. Here we focused on content property. We have to place all the elements we needed in the form inside it.

Learn SAP® UI5

Label

In the example, we need to add a label. We can search for label in explorer copy the detail and search it in API reference (library). In library, we will get a better view and in explorer, we will get examples. It is better to use API Reference (Library) because it has detailed information like how to use it. Inside the content add the label with the property text (Simple text is the text we are using).

Adding Simple Input

We already have seen use of sap.m.Input with parameters. If you don't know how to put the parameters, you can search it in the API Reference for properties. Copy and paste the sap.m.Input and check if possible to use it in the *placeholder* property. You will find that it will not show any properties because it might be inherited from its parent class, which are available in the class sap.m.InputBase containing the getPlaceHolder and setPlaceHolder property. We can also verify this in console.If we open up the console and check by creating an object for *sap.m.Input* by entering '*i = new sap.m.input*()'. Then check for the placeholder property by entering the 'i.setPlaceHolder' it will confirm that the property value can be used. In cases where you see it as undefined or null that mean we cannot use it that property. So back to the IDE and use the placeholder property for the sap.m.Input. Many a times, the properties are not found in the library, but are present in its super class.

Press Me Button

We need to add a button. For this, we use 'sap.m.Button' with the text property with the value 'Press Me'.

Rating

Search it from the explorer if we have something related to rating. Here we need a rating indicator. Click on it and see how it looks like. We can use this component for our rating part of the requirement. So copy the detail 'sap.m.Indicator' and paste it inside the content. Next step will be to know, how to give stars here. Sometimes it is easier to find property to use in explorer as well. Here they have given the star rating using '*value = 3.7*'we can directly use that in our program. We don't need go in API reference because we already figured in the explorer about how to use it. However, you can still check in API reference and you will get more exposure to other properties as well. It is advisable to study all the components present in your library and have good idea about what can be done with them.

Text Area

Search for the text area in the explorer and see what are the properties of text area for example does it have a placeholder? Moreover, question similar to that we can verify in console as well. We have a *value* property here so we need to use that to write content inside text area.

Add Date Picker

We are going to add the date picker. Search it in the explorer and then we are going to add that to our IDE. We do not have any value property here. So let keep it blank.

Learn SAP® UI5

File Browser

The next component we have to add is the File browser. Check if we can find that in the explorer. Now add it in the application without any properties values passed onto it. It will add a simple file uploader to your application.

Bar with a Button on Right hand side

The next thing we see in the form is a bar. We can get it by searching 'Bar' in the explorer. For the purpose of creating our form, we need to have a component bar. Inside this bar to add component we have to use content with a button on right side. Add a button using 'sap.m.Button'. The button has a property text with *value* as 'Right Side'.

VBOX Button

VBOX we will not find in the explorer. But we do have an element in UI5 library called VBOX. It allows aligning the contents in a vertical alignment (on top of each other).

HBOX Button

HBOX is similar to VBOX it will align the contents in Horizontal manner. Here we added two buttons inside the content of HBOX to align the buttons horizontally. You can get more information about the VBOX and HBOX in API reference and it will be very frequently used in applications.

You can verify if the 'item' aggregation is possible inside the VBOX. Run the console window and create an object for 'sap.m.VBox' and check if the 'item' aggregation is possible by simply type it there. Using the text property, we will give the name to the buttons 'VBOX Btn1' and 'VBOX Btn2'. The same way we can create 'HBOX' as well.

Finally, we can place the form content section. We are not going to create app or form. We can directly put it inside our 'div' by using 'oSimpleForm.placeAt("content")' at the end. If we run the application then we will get the result that we are expecting and shown in the above screenshot of the form.

You can also check our SAPUI5 Professional Development video course for accelerated learning: here or use the below QR code.

Learn SAP® UI5

SAP - Learn SAPUI5 Professional Development
UI5 Community Network • SAP Experts · SAP Services, SAP Consulting, SAP Education

Learn SAP UI5 / OpenUI5 In Detail: Basic & Advanced Levels, Step By Step, With The Help of The Best Open UI5 Experts

★★★★★ 4.5
(36 ratings)

56 lectures · 7 hours · Intermediate Level

Learn SAP® UI5

6. Data in UI5 Application

In this new section, we are going to see how data can be used in our UI5 application. We have already seen how to use components and how to create a basic application in UI5. We are going to work with JSON Data (Java Script Object Notation). If you have not worked with JSON before then below is a short introduction to JSON for beginner to JSON. If you are already familiar with it then you can skip to next subsection.

id	Name	waiting_number
A1	Ajay	1
A2	Jon	2
A3	Bob	3

```
[
    {
        "id": "A1",
        "Name": "Ajay",
        "waiting_number": 1
    },
    {
        "id": "A2",
        "Name": "Jon",
        "waiting_number": 2
    },
    {
        "id": "A3",
        "Name": "Bob",
        "waiting_number": 3
    }
]
```

In our database, we represent data in form of table and if we represent this table, which is having three columns named as id, Name and waiting number in JSON format. Here each row in the table represents one data set. Now, if we see how this table can be represented in JSON format.

In the picture on the right side, we can see that each records into corresponding object. The records are enclosed in three curly braces. You can also see that each object have some repetitive values. For example: id, Name and waiting_number. These are called as 'Keys'. They represent the column value of database table. In the right hand side we have A1,A2 and A3 as id values Ajay, Jon and Bob as Name values and 1, 2, 3 for waiting_number values. These are the actual data you work with it. Therefore, this is the simple JSON format representation of the table.

To use JSON data inside our UI5 Project. We have to create an object and we call that object as a 'Model'. Then we have to attach the models to view, so that they consume the data inside the model. To implement this in your UI5 Application is very simple.

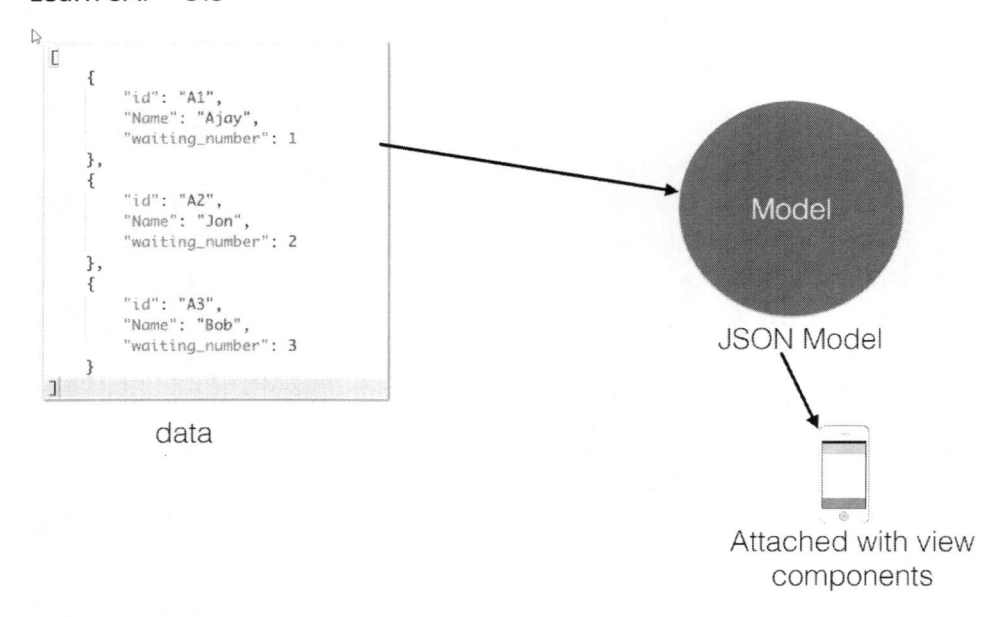

Learn SAP® UI5

```
[
    {
        "id": "A1",
        "Name": "Ajay",
        "waiting_number": 1
    },
    {
        "id": "A2",
        "Name": "Jon",
        "waiting_number": 2
    },
    {
        "id": "A3",
        "Name": "Bob",
        "waiting_number": 3
    }
]
```

data

Model

JSON Model

Attached with view components

First of all you have to assign the JSON data into *oData* variable and we are going to create an object of the model. The object of the model can be created by using 'new sap.ui.model.json.JSONModel()'. Once you are able to create an object of JSON Model you can use the function called 'setData' and put the JSON Data inside it. Once you are able to put the JSON Data inside our model object, then we will be able to use the model object in our application to use those data.

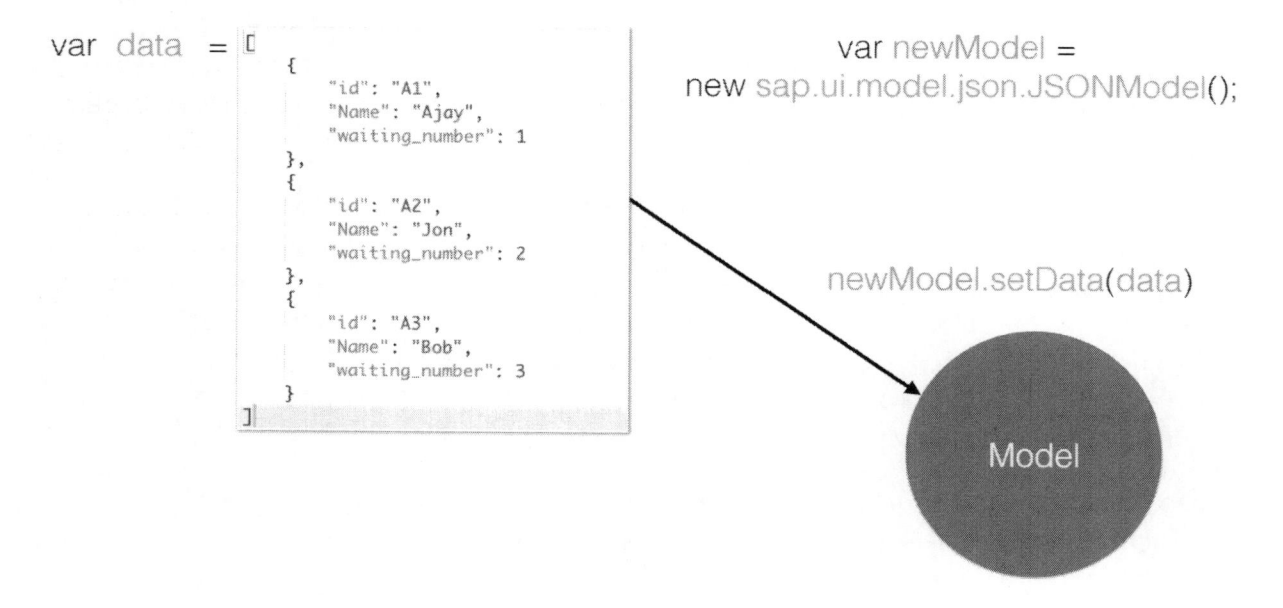

```
var data = [
    {
        "id": "A1",
        "Name": "Ajay",
        "waiting_number": 1
    },
    {
        "id": "A2",
        "Name": "Jon",
        "waiting_number": 2
    },
    {
        "id": "A3",
        "Name": "Bob",
        "waiting_number": 3
    }
]
```

var newModel = new sap.ui.model.json.JSONModel();

newModel.setData(data)

Model

To use this model object inside our application it consist of getting the element or component you want to put your data. And using the function 'setModel' you can assign the model to element or component. Once you do that, the element will be able to pick the data.

40

Learn SAP® UI5

```
                              var objectOfComponent =
                        sap.ui.getCore().byId("idOfComponent")

         Model


     newModel          objectOfComponent.setModel(newModel)
```

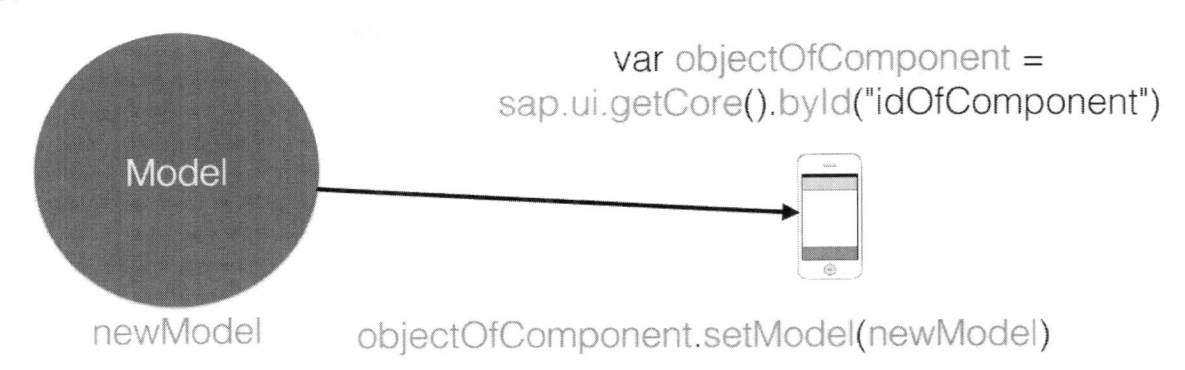

Two way binding

One of the other term we come across is *two -way binding*. Whenever we are binding the data to an element or component through our model, on changing the data or elements the model data will also be also changed. So this has a two way effect. For example, if you consider your element as your 'destination' and the data present in the model 'source'. By changing the data in the source, the data in the destination also changed and also by changing the data in the destination, the source data also changes. This is the concept of *two- way Binding*. We are going to see these concepts in action in out next section.

Now let us see how to accomplish this using UI5 lib.

Now if we go to our *model_demo_basic_1.html* code inside our clou9 editor then, you can see here the structure is pretty simple. We are having the script tab, which is including our UI5 libraries from 'openui5.hana.ondemand.com' with a blue crystal theme and we also including the 'sap.m' library.

These are very frequently used snippets. In the body, you can see a class called 'sapUiBody', which will be containing the app. This is the basic skeleton, which will load our UI5 library.

Here we creating two variables and those will be actually two labels of class 'sap.m.label'. With a text property.

```
<script>
        var label1 =new sap.m.Label({ /** creating path label1 */
            text:"{/key1}"           /** You need to use {/} for data
                                                            binding*/
        });
        var label2 =new sap.m.Label({ /**creating path label2 */
            text:"{/key2}"
        });
    var oData = {
        "key1":"Dinosars",          /* JSON Data for key 1
        "key2":"Elephant"           /* JSON Data for key 2*/
    };
    var newModel = new sap.ui.model.json.JSONModel();
    oModel.setData(oData);          /* Adding oData to a model */
    oLabel1.setModel(oModel);       /*Model is binded with element(oLabel1)
                                    */
    oLabel2.setModel(oModel); /*Model is binded with element (oLabel2) */
```

Learn SAP® UI5

```
        oLabel1.placeAt("content");    /* Using placeAt() function placing the
                                          label 1 content at HTML Page */
        oLabel2.placeAt("content1");   /* Using placeAt() function placing the
                                          label 1 content at HTML Page */
</script>
```

In the above program, we created a label1 with the text property and label2 with a text property. Once we created the object of label, then we add JSON data key inside '{}' which will be replaced by actual data values of JSON, once we bind the data either to global model or to individual elements. Finally, we place the labels in our HTML Page using 'placeAt' function. The content is going to be a part of div, if we save and run the live preview, we will see the below result:

Simple Tiles

DinosarsElephant

You can also check our SAPUI5 Professional Development video course for accelerated learning: here or use the below QR code.

Learn SAP® UI5

SAP - Learn SAPUI5 Professional Development
UI5 Community Network • SAP Experts - SAP Services, SAP Consulting, SAP Education

Learn SAP UI5 / OpenUI5 In Detail: Basic & Advanced Levels, Step By Step, With The Help of The Best Open UI5 Experts

★★★★★ 4.5
(36 ratings)

● 56 lectures ⓒ 7 hours ⫶ Intermediate Level

Learn SAP® UI5

7. List

In this section, we are going to see, one of most popular UI5 element and that is *List*. To use List in our application, we have to use 'sap.m.List'.

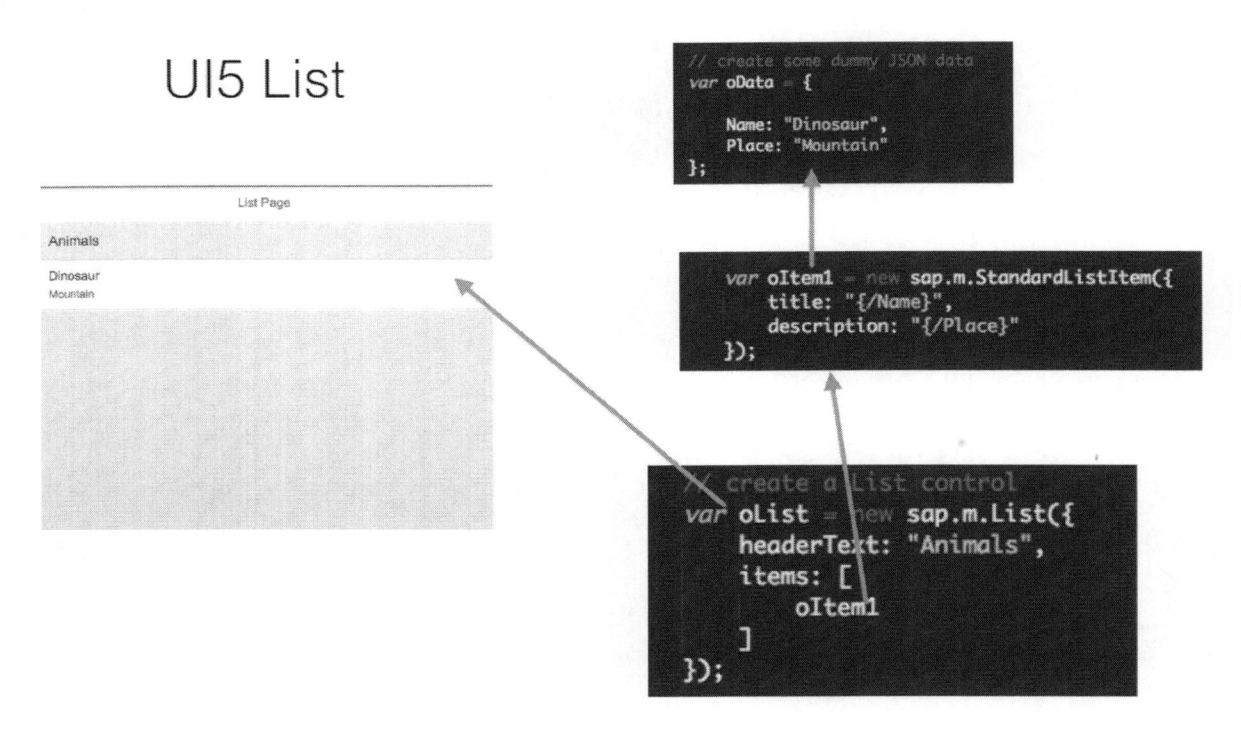

UI5 List

```javascript
// create some dummy JSON data
var oData = {
    Name: "Dinosaur",
    Place: "Mountain"
};
```

```javascript
var oItem1 = new sap.m.StandardListItem({
    title: "{/Name}",
    description: "{/Place}"
});
```

```javascript
// create a List control
var oList = new sap.m.List({
    headerText: "Animals",
    items: [
        oItem1
    ]
});
```

Let us create a simple list and show one single item as 'dinosaur' with a description 'mountain' inside the list.

Steps to create a list

1. The first step is to create standard list item. Once we have a standard list items those are the items that will be present inside our list.

2. Second step is to create a list object using 'sap.m.List'. Once we created the 'sap.m.list', we can put the standard items inside the list. Here dinosaur is a list item and animal is a list.

3. The third step is providing the data. In the picture you might notice the use of curly braces with backslash '{/}'. This represents the data binding.

Now, if we go to our cloud 9 *program list_demo_basic_3.html*, to see how to implement this list. We can find below structure:

```
<script id='sap-ui-bootstrap' type='text/javascript'
src='https://openui5.hana.ondemand.com/resources/sap-ui-core.js'data-sap-ui-theme='sap_bluecrystal'           data-sap-ui-libs='sap.m'
</script>
```

Learn SAP® UI5

In this application, we are going to use 'sap.m.App' and 'sap.m.Page' as well. First, we create a page and app using below code:

```
var oPage = new sap.m.Page({            /** Creating a page using oPage
                                                                      */
        title: "List Page",
        content: [
            oList
        ]
});
    var oApp = new sap.m.App({          /** Creating an App using oApp */
        pages: [oPage]
}).placeAt("content");                  /** Place the content in HTML*/
```

We also have to create the content. For that inside the body tags create a div element and add the content. Now we have the page and list ready. Next, we are going to add a list.

Next, we need to create the data. Create the oData object and add the data inside the JSON data. In previous data binding example we have only data present, for creating simple app. Now we are going to add more data. Therefore, what we are going to do is create a names property inside the oData and all the data can be put inside it.

```
var oData = {
names:[{
    Name: "Dinosaur",
    Place: "Mountain"
}, {
    Name: "Elephant",
    Place: "Forest"
}, {
    Name: "Whale",
    Place: "Sea"
}, {
    Name: "Duck",
    Place: "Water"
}, {
    Name: "Monkey",
    Place: "Tree"

}]

};
```

In the above example, we added a *name* key, which is an array. Each array contains object in it and each object are single records. Next, we are going to create a list. For this, we use the bind item aggregation.

```
// bind the oList items to the oData collection
    oList.bindItems({
        path: "/names",
        template: new sap.m.StandardListItem({
            title: "{Name}",
            description: "{Place}"
```

Learn SAP® UI5

```
            })
        });
```

Here the '`path: "/names"`' specifies the data which is pointing to the path.

The second parameter is the template. It is the standard template of the list item. It will act as a blueprint for the list items. First, we created a page after that we add some data using oData and then finally, we bind the data with list.

If you are using eclipse and there are separate view-controller then, all the parts will be performed in controllers like data binding, process of data and operations related to it.

Now if we run the code and see the result, we will see below output:

List Page
Animals
Dinosaur Mountain
Elephant Forest
Whale Sea
Duck Water
Monkey Tree

Here, we have made the creation of standard list items generic and all the items are taken from JSON data and added to our final list, which you can see in output.

You can also check our SAPUI5 Professional Development video course for accelerated learning: here or use the below QR code.

Learn SAP® UI5

SAP - Learn SAPUI5 Professional Development
UI5 Community Network • SAP Experts · SAP Services, SAP Consulting, SAP Education

Learn SAP UI5 / OpenUI5 In Detail: Basic & Advanced Levels, Step By Step, With The Help of The Best Open UI5 Experts

★★★★★ 4.5
(36 ratings)

● 56 lectures ⏲ 7 hours ⋮⋮⋮ Intermediate Level

Learn SAP® UI5

8. Table

Table is the most used elements in UI5 Library. The structure of the table is similar to excel sheets we work with. In a table, we have a header, which contains the title and we have rows, which contain data. Below are simplified step to create a table with UI5.

1. The first step is defining and creating columns.

2. The second step is to add the columns to the table.

3. The third step is to define how the rows will look like. Here we use 'sap.m.ColumnListItem'. So each individual record is treated as an individual list item.

4. In the final step we will bind the table with data.

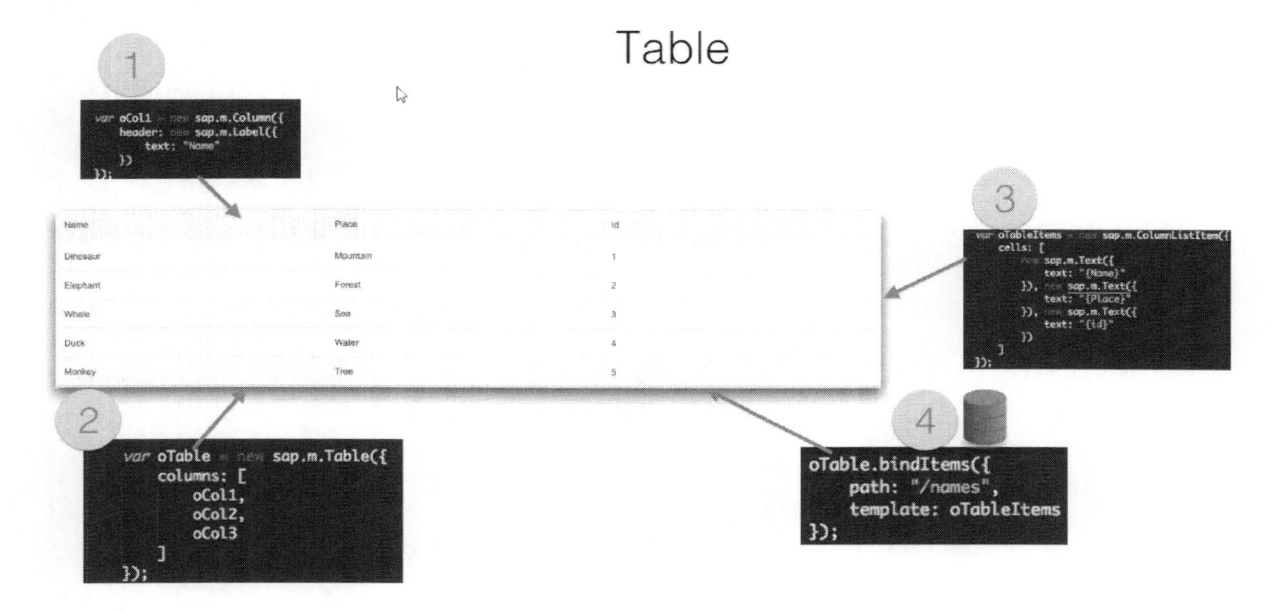

Table

```
1
var oCol1 = new sap.m.Column({
    header: new sap.m.Label({
        text: "Name"
    })
});
```

Name	Place	Id
Dinosaur	Mountain	1
Elephant	Forest	2
Whale	Sea	3
Duck	Water	4
Monkey	Tree	5

```
3
var oTableItems = new sap.m.ColumnListItem({
    cells: [
        new sap.m.Text({
            text: "{Name}"
        }),
        new sap.m.Text({
            text: "{Place}"
        }),
        new sap.m.Text({
            text: "{id}"
        })
    ]
});
```

```
2
var oTable = new sap.m.Table({
    columns: [
        oCol1,
        oCol2,
        oCol3
    ]
});
```

```
4
oTable.bindItems({
    path: "/names",
    template: oTableItems
});
```

Below is the code, to create a simple 'sap.m.Table' .Initially we define data and model.

```
var oModel = new sap.ui.model.json.JSONModel();// creating a Model
                                                with this data
```

Then we need to create three columns with name, place and id labels. Create an oCol object for the label.

```
var oCol1 = new sap.m.Column({ // creating column 1 object for name
        header:new sap.m.Label({"Name"})
    }),
    var oCol2 = new sap.m.Column({// creating column2 object for Place
        header:new sap.m.Label({"Place"})
    }),

});
    var oCol3 = new sap.m.Column({// creating column3 object for Id
        header:new sap.m.Label({"Id"})
```

Learn SAP® UI5

});

After that, we add column to the table

```
var oTable = new sap.m.Table({
title:"Simple Table",
columns:[
        oCol1
oCol2
        oCol3
        ]
})
```

Now we need to define how the rows will be by creating a template.

```
var oTemp = new sap.m.ColumnListItem({
     cells:[
     new sap.m.Text({
            text:"{Name}"
         }),
     new sap.m.Text({
            text:"{Place}"
         }),
     new sap.m.Text({
            text:"{id}"
         })
     ]
})
```

Finally, we do the data binding steps, where we provide the data path to the 'oTemp'. In this case, the individual list items will be generated based on the data.

```
oTable.bindItems({
       path: "/names",
       template: oTemp
       })
```

In the previous section we saw, when we are working with MVC Pattern, the data and model related activity should be in the controller. Place the data and model activity inside the onInit() function of the controller as it should be executed when the program starts execution. One more thing we have to do is assign the model to global model. Once you set this, then data can be accessible from anywhere in the application. Below is the code to do that.

```
sap.ui.getCore().setModel(oModel);
```

Now when you save and run the application. You will get the desired output, which is shown above in the image.

Table using:sap.ui.commons

There are a lot of variations and properties, which are given out of box with UI5 library. One such example is use of 'sap.ui.commons' table. Below are the steps to perform to create a

Learn SAP® UI5

table with commons. If we reuse the code of 'sap.m.Table' then, the first thing to change is index.html file where we have to add two additional libraries, as shown below.

```
<script src="resources/sap-ui-core.js"
        id="sap-ui-bootstrap"
  data-sap-ui-libs="sap.m,sap.ui.commons,sap.ui.table"  //Added additionally
                                              sap.ui.commons and sap.ui.table
        data-sap-ui-theme="sap_bluecrystal">
</script>
```

The in view we have to change the type of the coloums:

```
var oCol1 = new sap.ui.table.Column({
        label: new sap.m.Label({
            text: "Name"
        }),
        template: new sap.m.Text({
            text: "{Name}"
        })
    });
var oCol2 = new sap.ui.table.Column({
        label: new sap.m.Label({
            text: "Place"
        }),
        template: new sap.m.Text({
            text: "{Place}"
        })
    });
var oCol3 = new sap.ui.table.Column({
        label: new sap.m.Label({
            text: "Id"
        }),
```

Finally, in binding, we can use one simpler version of binding. This is called 'bindrows'. As we already defined template in column level, so we do not need to create that separately.

```
oList.bindItems("/names");
```

These are the simple changes to be made for our new table variant. Now run this application and you can see the difference between the old and new table.

Simple Table

Name	Place	Id
Dinosaurs	Mountain	Mountain
Elephant	Forest	Forest
Whale	Sea	Sea
Duck	Water	Water
Monkey	Tree	Tree

Learn SAP® UI5

Here the structure is changed and it is responsive to the mobile devices as well up to certain extent. Nevertheless, the main decision to select which table (sap.m and sap.ui) to use, depends on two factors:
- Functionalities.
- And main target device type.

You can also check our SAPUI5 Professional Development video course for accelerated learning: here or use the below QR code.

Learn SAP® UI5

9. Tiles

Tiles are wonderful way of providing multiple features, which are logically separated. They are also popular in showing KPI information data as well.
There are two simple steps to create tiles:

1. Create individual tiles.
2. Add these tiles to a tile container.

Now let us try a simple scenario for creating tiles and add these tiles in a tile container. In the cloud9 shared workspace you can see 'tile_demo_basic_1&2.html'. The steps mentioned are simple; we create individual tiles using 'StandardTile':

```
var oT1 = new sap.m.StandardTile({
    title: "Dinosaur",
    info: "Mountain"
    icon: "sap-icon://sap-ui5"
});
```

This is the one tile created for Dinosaur. Similar way we can create other tiles and name them oT2, oT3 and oT4. Inside tiles, it contains properties like *title*, *info* and *icon*. In the *icon* property, we need to specify the icon we are going to use. For this, we can search in UI5 icon explorer in URL https://openui5.hana.ondemand.com/iconExplorer.html. Here select the icon you want to add and copy the name of the icon and paste it inside the icon property.

Next, create tile container and add these tiles to the container.

```
var oTileCont = new sap.m. oTileContainer({
    tiles: [
        oT1,
        oT2,
        oT3,
        oT4
    ]
});
```

Then place this oTileContto the page:

```
Var page =new sap.m.Page({
    title: "Simple Tiles",
    content: [
        oTileCont
    ]
})
```

Save and run, if everything is works fine. You will see below output:

52

Learn SAP® UI5

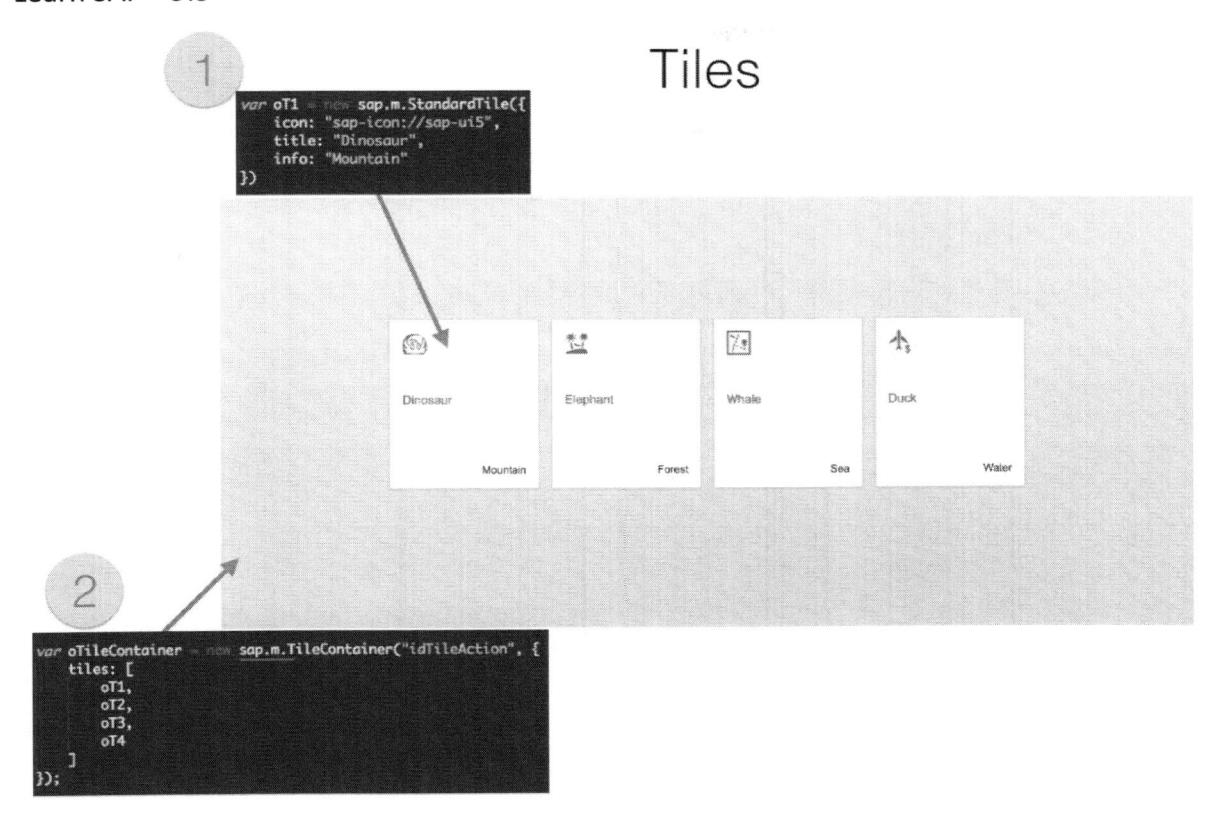

Tiles

```
var oT1 = new sap.m.StandardTile({
    icon: "sap-icon://sap-ui5",
    title: "Dinosaur",
    info: "Mountain"
})
```

```
var oTileContainer = new sap.m.TileContainer("idTileAction", {
    tiles: [
        oT1,
        oT2,
        oT3,
        oT4
    ]
});
```

Create Tiles Using Data Binding (JSON Data variable)

If we have a data source and we want to use it for creating these tiles. Then we need to perform few changes. First step is to ensure all the data to bind is correct, as we are going to use an icon property, so data should contain that as well:

```
var oData = {
        "names" :[{
            icon : "sap-icon://sap-ui5",
            Name : "Dinosaur",
            Place : "Mountain"
        }, {
            icon : "sap-icon://general-leave-request",
            Name : "Elephant",
            Place : "Forest"
        }, {
            icon : "sap-icon://map-2",
            Name : "Whale",
            Place : "Sea"
        }, {
            icon : "sap-icon://travel-expense",
            Name : "Duck",
            Place : "Water"
        }]
    };
    var oModel = new sap.ui.model.json.JSONModel(oData);
```

53

Next, remove the hard coded part, as we are going to use data binding here:

```
var oTileTemplate = new sap.m.StandardTile({ //Creating template
icon: "{icon}",
          title: "{Name}",
info: "{Place}"

});


var oTileContainer = new sap.m.TileContainer("idTileAction", {

});


oTileContainer.bindAggregation("tiles", "/names", oTileTemplate);
//Bind aggregation parameters contain (property,/path and template)

oTileContainer.setModel(oModel);

var page = new sap.m.Page({
          title: "Simple Tile",
          enableScrolling: false,
          content: [
              oTileContainer
          ]
      });
var app = new sap.m.App();
app.addPage(page);
      app.placeAt("content");
```

This is the general way of creating simple tile without any hard coding. Hard coding should be avoided in project. While using tiles in real projects as well, we should use bind aggregation function. Below is the output, which our program results into:

Learn SAP® UI5

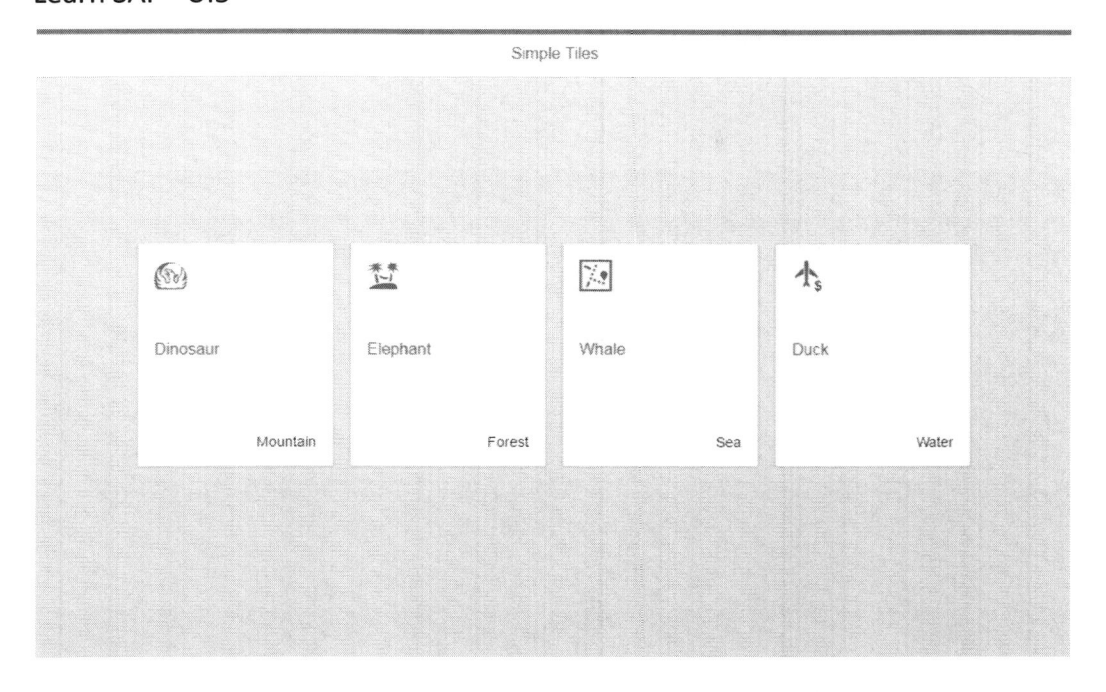

You can also check our SAPUI5 Professional Development video course for accelerated learning: here or use the below QR code.

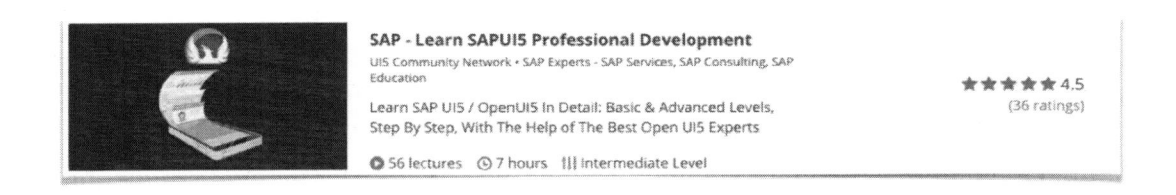

Learn SAP® UI5

10. Data Binding Using Factory Functions

If you are wondering, how the data binding is done internally then the concept of factory function will give you more clarity. Factory function is a way to implement custom logic while data binding is being performed.

For example, if we have a requirement where, we have a list and the description is dependent upon the title value. If main content of list is name of the animal and the description contains some dependency on it. Then factory functions are way to achieve those binding and make these general.

In our case, if we represent list title as animal name and we have to mention description if the animal is extinct or not. Then we need to use `bindAggregation` with an additional third parameter as custom function, which contains the logic of returning animal specific description. Below is the picture of how the code and output will look like:

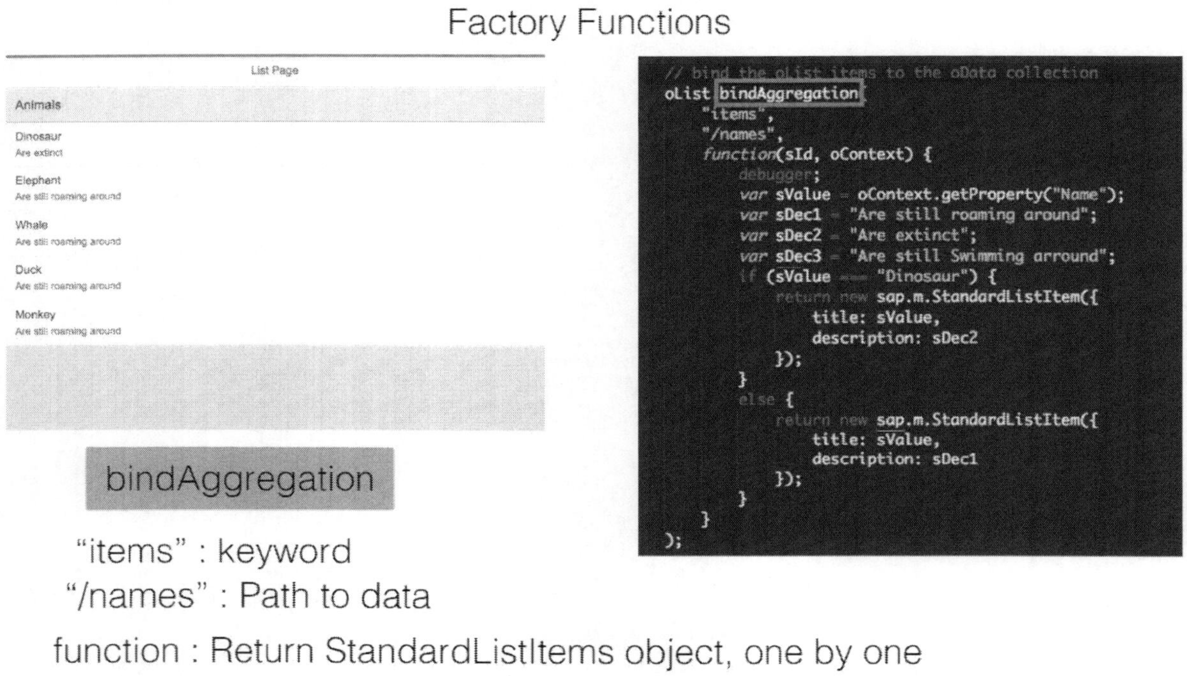

Factory Functions

"items" : keyword
"/names" : Path to data
function : Return StandardListItems object, one by one

The third parameter of `bindAggregation` function is going to be custom function, which takes two parameters. First is `sId` and other is `oContext`. Parameter oContextwill contain all the necessary information, which you require for your operation:

```
oList.bindAggregation("items",
            "/names",
            function(sId,oContext){
        var sValue = oContext.getProperty("Name");
        var sDesc1 = "Are still roaming around"; //String Description
        var sDesc2 = "Are Extinct"//String Description

            });
if(sValue === "Dinosaur"){   //If stmt to tell the desc is extinct
    return new sap.m.StandardListItem({
        title:sValue,
```

56

Learn SAP® UI5

```
                description:sDec2
    });
} else {
    returnnew sap.m.StandardListItem({
        title:sValue,
        description:sDesc1

    });
}
```

You can also add a debugger to debug the code by adding the 'debugger' keyword in the code. After adding the debugger inside your code, if you open the development kit (Firefox and Chrome) then you can even analyse more about behavior of the code.

NAMED MODEL

The next topic we are going to see is named model. Previously we were having the JSON Data and setting the model with JSON Data. Then we set that model to the Core. Now the question comes here -can we have more than data object set to my core. And for your surprise, yes we can. Using the concept of named model.
Previously we use the 'sap.ui.getCore().setModel(oModel)'. This model was set to the core and can be referred to the global model. However, when we are using the concept of named model we have to provide a second argument. The second argument is actually the name of the argument we are setting up. For example *XYZ, ABC* or any name. This name should be a valid string character. When we are passing the model object and the name of the model then this model object can only be retrieved with this name. It will act as a key for this model.

Global/Core Model syntax (example): sap.ui.getCore().setModel(oModel)
Named Model syntax (example): sap.ui.getCore().setModel(oModel,XYZ)

Next question, which comes, is how to use the named model in data binding? Below is a simple comparison between the named model and normal model binding we were doing previously. In case of names model we will be using '>' operator to separate the name of the model and key value in binding, as shown below:

Normal Model
```
        oList.Items({
path: "/names",
template:new sap.m.StandardListItem({
        title:"{Name}" // No greater than symbols for Normal Model
description:"{Place}",
        type: sap.m.ListType.Navigation,
        press: [oController.showDetails, oController]
})
    });
```

Learn SAP® UI5

Named Model

```
       oList.Items({
path: "XYZ>/names",//Greater than symbol to represent Named Model
template:new sap.m.StandardListItem({
              title:"{XYZ>Name}"      //Greater than symbol to represent
                                                          Named Model
           description:"{XYZ>Place}",  //Greater than symbol to represent
                                                          Named Model

        type: sap.m.ListType.Navigation,
        press: [oController.showDetails, oController]
})
      });
```

While you are using the named model you have to specify name with greater than symbol before using the keys. For example: `title:"{XYZ>Name}"`.

Note: Always try to use the Global/Core Model and try to restrict the as much as you can for named model. While you are creating multiple named models it becomes very complex to track how many number of Named Mode actually exists.

You can also check our SAPUI5 Professional Development video course for accelerated learning: here or use the below QR code.

Learn SAP® UI5

11. Using Chrome Development Toolkit

In this section, we are going to see how Google Chrome development kit can help us speed our development. Google chrome is one of the best browsers out there in the marketplace. If you are developing any application, which is related to web, then Google Chrome is going to be the first preference. Chrome provides a lot of out of the box features that will be very useful for a developer. Not only for development but also for finding bugs, analysing style sheets and correcting them on the fly. We will see the features of Google Chrome browsers one by one.

Note: If you have to deliver the application to the customer and your customers are not using Google Chrome and might be using Firefox or Internet explorer. Then you have to check the application that your customer is using and check if everything is working or compatible with that browser before delivering the application. Sometimes many features are not compatible across browsers.

Let's look into the features of Google Chrome. You have to click 'F12' in window machine or simply right click and select inspect element. Now development toolkit can placed in right hand side or below the browser or you can even separate the development kit window from *customize and control* functionality present at top right corner.

The separate window layout will be very useful when you have dual screens setup. For now let's dock it in the right hand side of the browser screen.

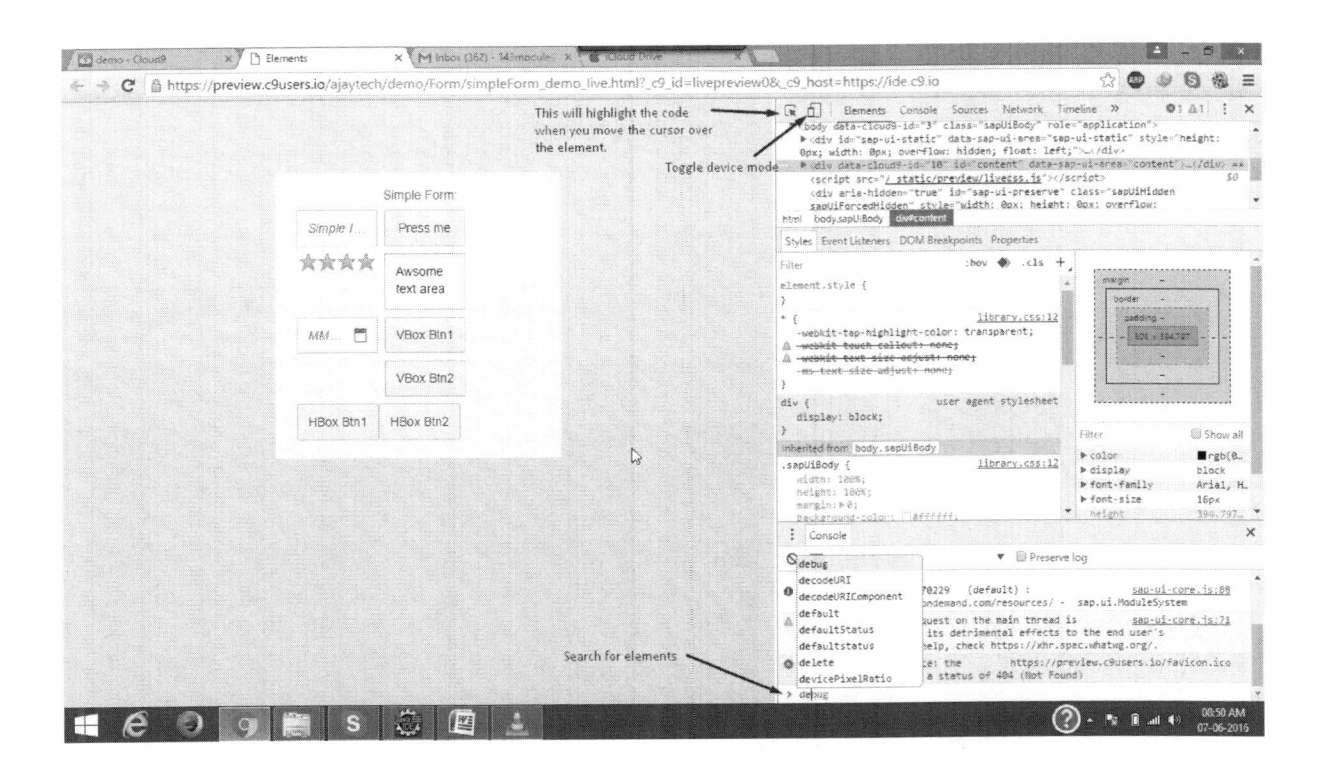

Now let us have a walk though of different tabs present.

59

Elements tab

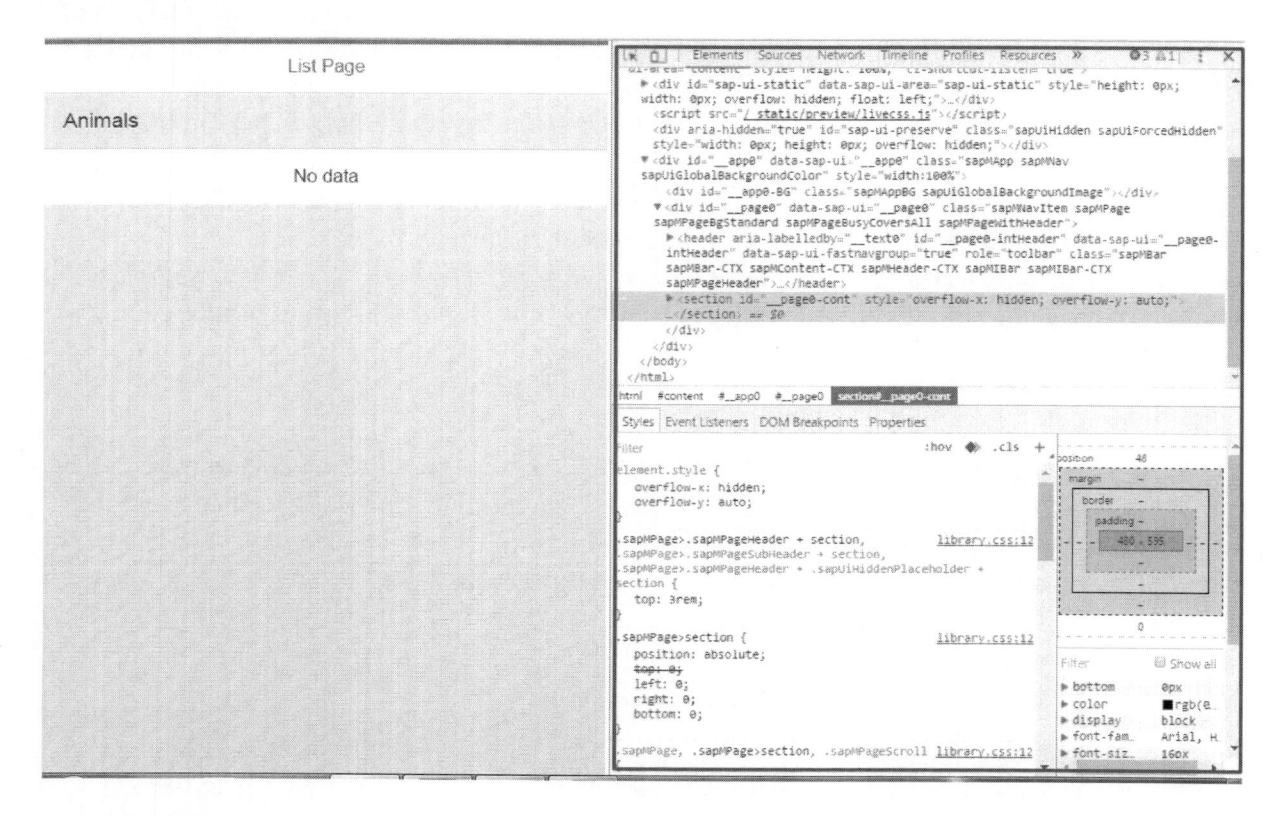

It provides all the HTML elements in a tree format. If we collapse the entire tree, we can see which is the root element is which is HTML in this case. You can also expand and see what the elements inside the tree are. There are lots of components, which are available. Sometimes, it is very difficult to find these elements. Therefore, you can use search here.

Search

Press 'Ctrl+F' in window machine or 'Command+F' in MAC. If you want to search and find an element then, you can simply search in the bar by typing in the name of the component or even any property or any relative value you know which will match the element.
If we search for the submit button. It will highlight the component in yellow color. This is very handy when you are looking for a component in your web page. One more option is there if you want to check for a component that is repeated in the application. Then enter the component and clicks enter every time it will show you where in other places also it is used. You can also press 'Ctrl+Z' to go back to your previous search.
 One handier feature is the **selection element** feature. Once you select this, it will turn into blue. When you move the mouse over the screen then the particular 'div' element is highlighted in the screen.

Learn SAP® UI5

Change HTML on the Fly

If you want to change the HTML then you can right click and select 'Edit as HTML'. Now you can do changes to your DOM Elements. If we delete the entire element then the particular section will be removed from the web page instantly.

CSS Properties

```
html ...
Styles  Event Listeners  DOM Breakpoints  Properties
Filter                          :hov      .cls  +
element.style {
    height: 100%;
}
html[data-sap-ui-              library.css:12
animation='on'] {
}
.sapUiTheme-sap_bluecrystal    library.css:12
{
    font-size: 16px;
}
* {                            library.css:12
```

CSS are very powerful tool. When you highlight some **DOM** elements then you can see the CSS properties linked to that in right hand side. Here we can perform changes in the CSS properties like color, padding, width etc. directly and that will be reflected instantly on the web page.

When you have a requirement to do lot of design changes in CSS then changing CSS and seeing the result on the fly is essential. For example if your customer asks you to change, the color of the button or the button needs to be presented at the bottom of the page. The CSS Style tab provides lot of trial and error approach to reach to final optimum CSS code to achieve that.

For example to change the background color of Input we select the input and give the class name with `background-color` property .Note here that, if there are some properties that are overwritten by other properties then according to precedence the final result will be shown. If you mention it as important then the mentioned value will have the higher priority.

Learn SAP® UI5

Toggle Device Mode

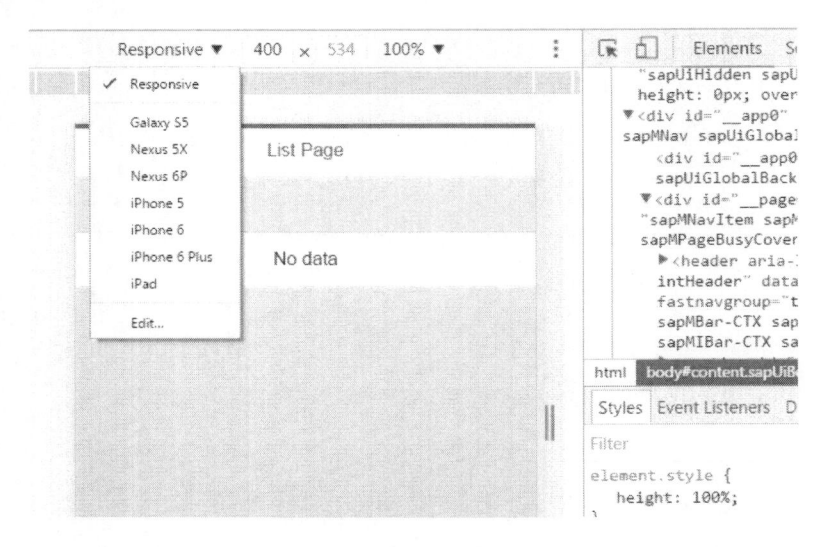

In toggle device mode, you can view the application of how it will looks like in other devices like iPhone, Nexus 6 and more. There is also one edit tab as well. This will allow you to choose the devices available in the list.

BROWSER CONSOLE

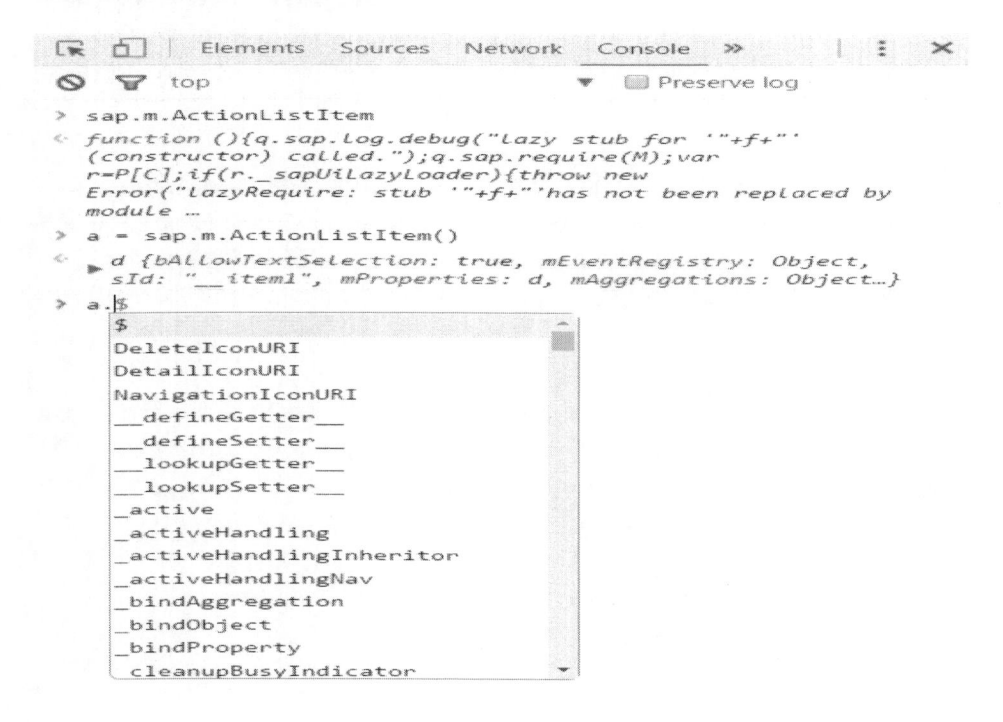

Learn SAP® UI5

Console is like a real-time editor of your web page. When you are loading an application then if there are some errors and your application is not loading properly. Then the console is the place where you will find what the errors are.
This also provides a brief log of your application runtime. This will provide what are the libraries that are loaded which application started running and when.

We can also write code in our console. When you write a code in console, you will get real time feedback for it. You instantly know if particular code is going to work in our application or not. To try that now we are going to clear the console using 'clear()' function.

Source

This tab provides capability to debug our application, see code and file involved in our application .The left side bar will give the glimpse of all the files, which are involved in our project. For example if we want to debug the view file then we can select the view file and fix a debug point by pressing on the line number left to it. Then go to the console and refresh the page. It will stop you at the debugging point you fixed. The debugging point will be triggered only if the console window (development toolkit) is opened. The debugging point can be disabled by enabling the icon for 'Deactivate breaking points'

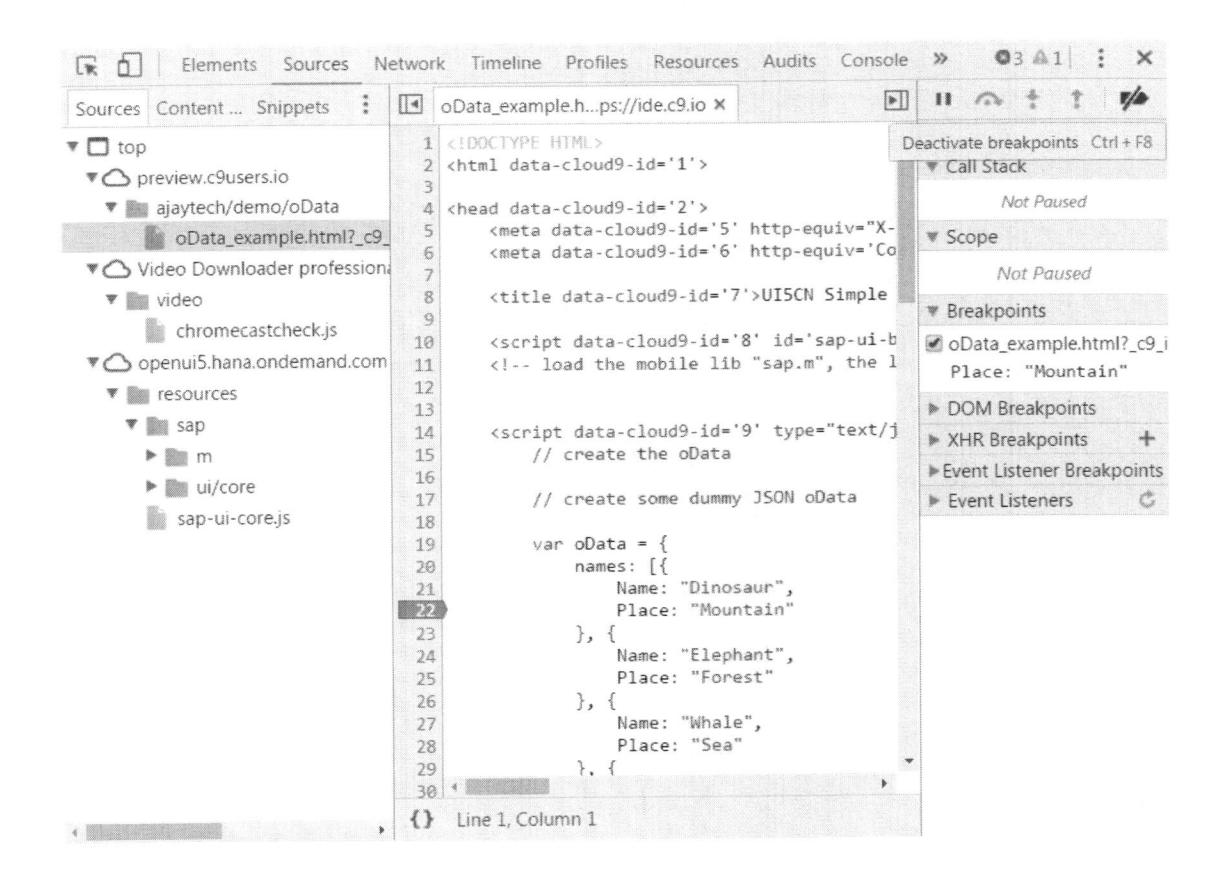

Learn SAP® UI5

Network

In the network tab you can see all the components that are loaded. If there are some components that are called from API then you can also see the status, check there request and response. If you want to see the data or response then click on it and you will be able to see the details in the response window.

The header section will gives you a glimpse of all the details like request method, request URL and the status code. These will be handy when you are debugging and can verify if all the API communications are carried out as expected. In addition, there is also a filter tab available where you can filter the contents using name and the type like CSS, JS, Image, media and much more.

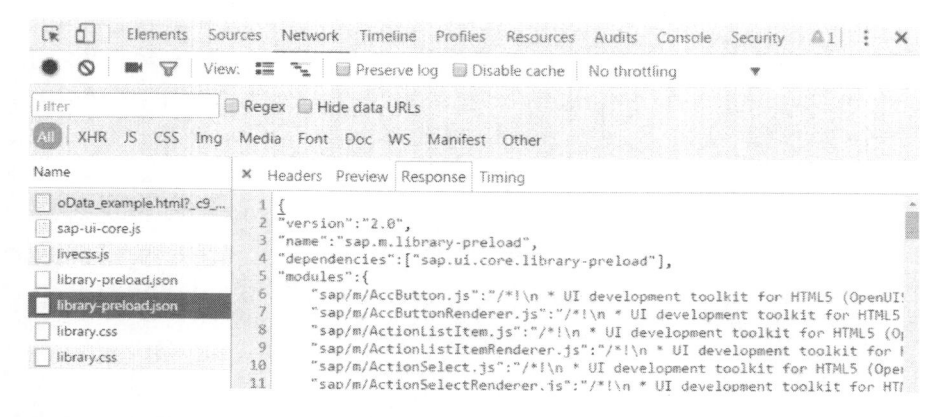

Responsiveness and Browser Compatibility

Responsiveness in UI5 Application can be a make or break decisions. When you deliver the product for user acceptance testing, they will test the applications in their own devices and environment. It can be a mobile device, tablet or desktop computer. So you need to create the applications depends upon what your used are going to use. In addition, the browser that user will use should be decided initially. Because there are many features, which may not supported in some browsers or work differently in different browsers and at later point of time change can result into major development.

You can check additional compatibility with browsers in API reference as well. There is a help section for developers in http://openui5.hana.ondemand.com, which gives details about browser and platform support guide.

To put concisely, always consider these three things before taking any major decision:

1. Know your customer devices and environment well.
2. Check compatibility rules from SAP help document for running environment.
3. Consider always the cross browser and devices usage in development phase.

12. Styling and Theming for UI5 App

The Styling and theming will make your webpage more responsive and presentable to your users. The responsiveness of your application is depends upon the media query. The media query is part of CSS. The CSS plays a major role in UI5 Applications. You may ask how much CSS we need to know, if we are creating end-to-end UI5 app, to answer this it is necessary to know CSS in detail.

Generally, in big UI5 projects there are two set of people. Those who are focuses on the development and other focusing on the design. The people who are working in design will focus on user experience and CSS. If the people are working in development, they are focusing on controller, view, data and UI5 Libraries.

We already have created one 'Simple APP' containing an input box and a button. We are going to see how to change CSS design so it look much nicer and also we are going to bring input box and button to centre in both mobile and desktop view of the application.

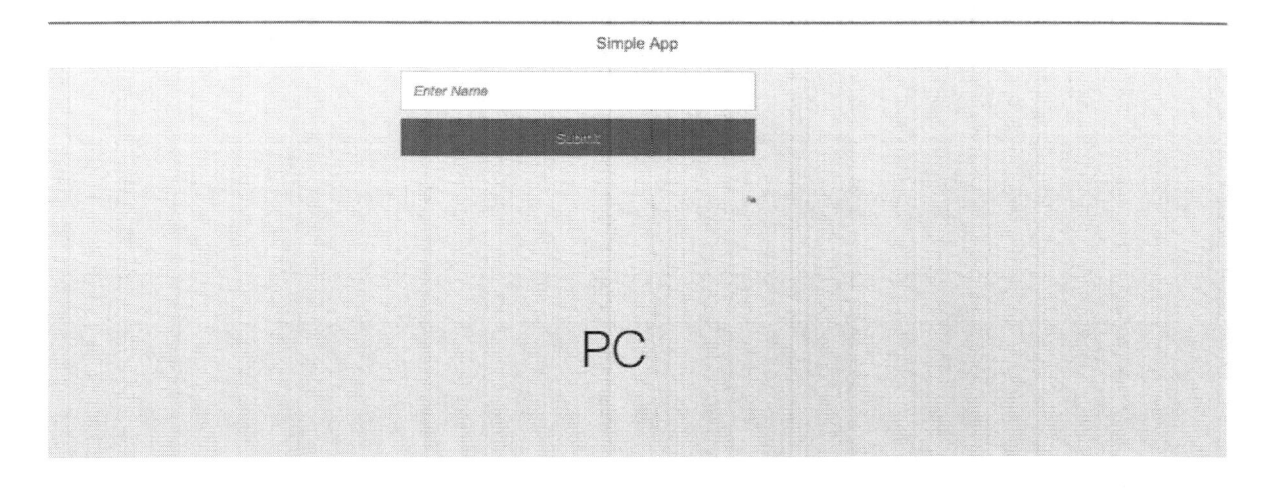

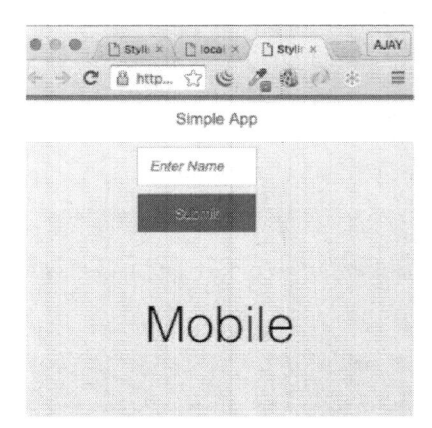

To start the process let us open our development toolkit. Now here we are going to use our element tab to do the changes. To focus on the input box right click on the input box and select inspect element. This will highlight the html content of the input in browser console.

Let's look for the class that is assigned to input element. Most of the standard CSS class starts with 'sap'. So be careful when you change the standard CSS class. Because, if you change the standard class it will be effected everywhere in the application. So better not to experiment with the standard classes.

Now I am going to create a custom class. For that in styles tab click the '+' sign to add a class (The highlighted class has been edited here).To this class add the width property and assign it 60% and padding left as 30%. We need our custom styling to be taken on highest presidency so we can add'! important' keyword after the style property value. We can see in output that the input box will be aligned to middle. Following the same steps, we can align our button to middle as well. Now, we need to take care of the blue background color for our button. This will be little tricky because, we have to involve standard style class '.sapMBtnInner' to make this changes. You will notice that if you add the property:

```
background: #007cc0;
```

inside class '.sapMBtnInner', then the background of the button will be changed. As we already know that changing the standard style class is not a good practice, so to achieve that we will create .btnCsscustom class. And we will write the styling rule in such a way that all the elements which are having both .sapMBtnInnerclass and .btnCss are going change with the new style rule. This is achieved by creating style rule inside selector :

```
.btnCss>.sapMBtnInner{
 }
```

Finally, this is how the CSS file will look like:

```
.inputCss{         //CSS class for input

    width: 60%!important;
padding-left: 30%!important;

}


.btnCss{           //CSS Class for button
     width: 60%!important;
padding-left: 30%!important;

}

 .btnCss>.sapMBtnInner{                   //Apply the property to the element
                                                              sapMBtnInner

    background: #007cc0;
}
```

to link this CSS file we can use `<link>` tag:

```
<linkrel="stylesheet"type="text/css"href="css/custom.css">
```

Now in view we have to use 'addStyleClass' function to link the new CSS properties as shown below:

```js
createContent : function(oController) {
        var oSimpleInput = new sap.m.Input({

            placeholder:"Enter Name"

        }).addStyleClass("inputCss");  //class for CSS
        var oBtn = new sap.m.Button({
            text:"Submit"
        }).addStyleClass("btnCss");   //Class for CSS
        var oPage = new sap.m.Page({
            title: "Simple App",
            content: [
                oSimpleInput,
                oBtn
            ]
        });
```

And once we run this code in our web browser, we will be able to achieve our desired output:

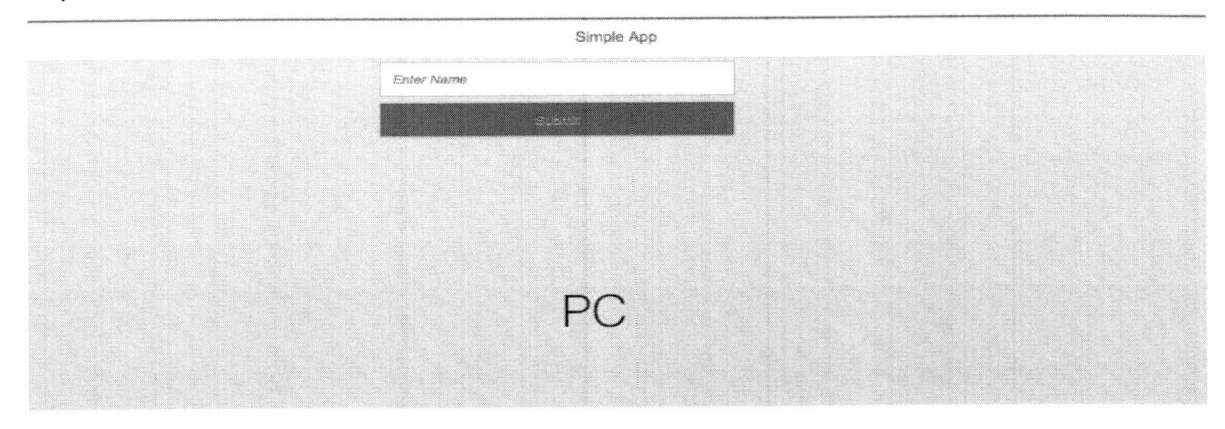

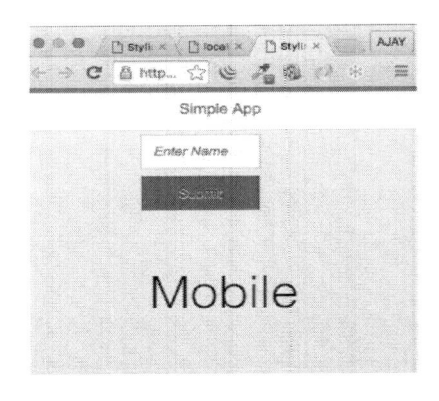

PC

Mobile

Learn SAP® UI5

Styling and Theming, advance options

Media Query

Media query gives you control on, how your application will look in different resolution screen. Such as mobile, tablet or desktop computer screen. Below is a simple example of media query:

```
@mediascreen and (max-width:600px){
     .hBoxForm{
     padding-left: 10%;
}
.vBoxForm{
          padding-left: 18%;

          }
}
```

In above CSS, the .hBoxForm and .vBoxForm are going be applied to only the screen which are having less than 600px width. Now you might be thinking that, this will result into a big and complex CSS file. That is true and the primary reason why CSS files in UI5 projects are generally large in size.

THEME DESIGNER

Imagine a tool, which will help you to reduce this tedious task of changing your application basic look and feel without much work. Theme designer is the tool to automate the tedious task of changing CSS. It is a 'What You See Is What You Get(WYSIWYG)' editor.

Browser-based, graphical "what you see is what you get(WYSIWYG)" editor

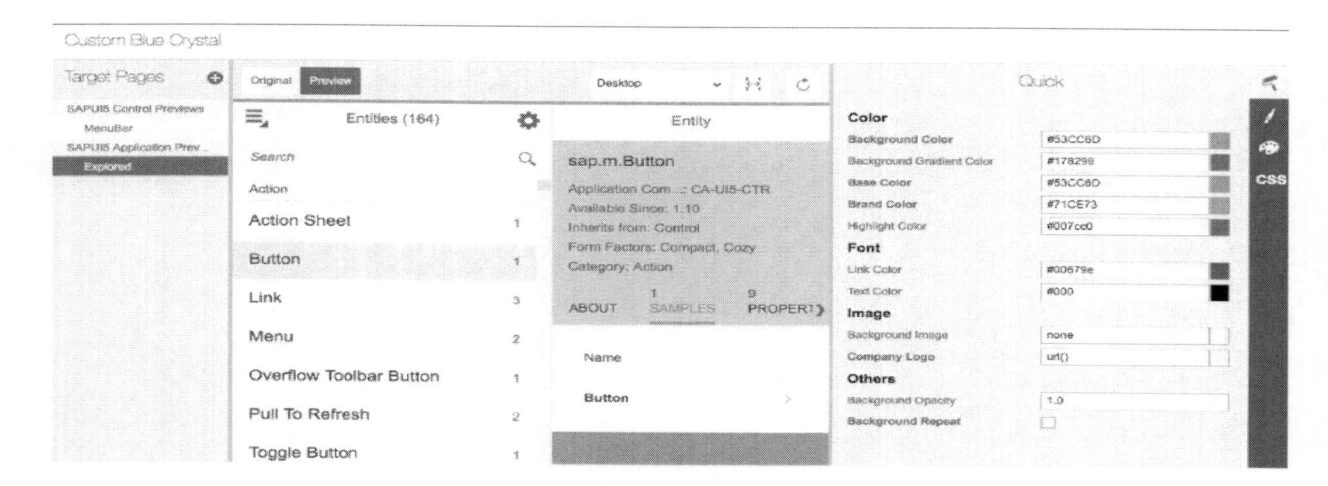

Learn SAP® UI5

You can see in above picture that, Theme designer will have a lot of in-build options in right hand side to change the color and basic appearance.

You can launch Theme designer from your SAP with the Transaction-code:

/UI5/THEME_DESIGNER

Alternatively, you can go directly to below URL to access this browser based graphical editor.

https://<server>:<port>/sap/bc/theming/theme-designer?sap-client=<client>

(You need to change server and port name here and replace with the Server and Port name of your SAP system).

Once you are finished with the design and changes then, you can see the list of themes available and you can import the theme. It will ask for a link. If you have an application running on SAP Server then you can use the link to open it in theme designer.

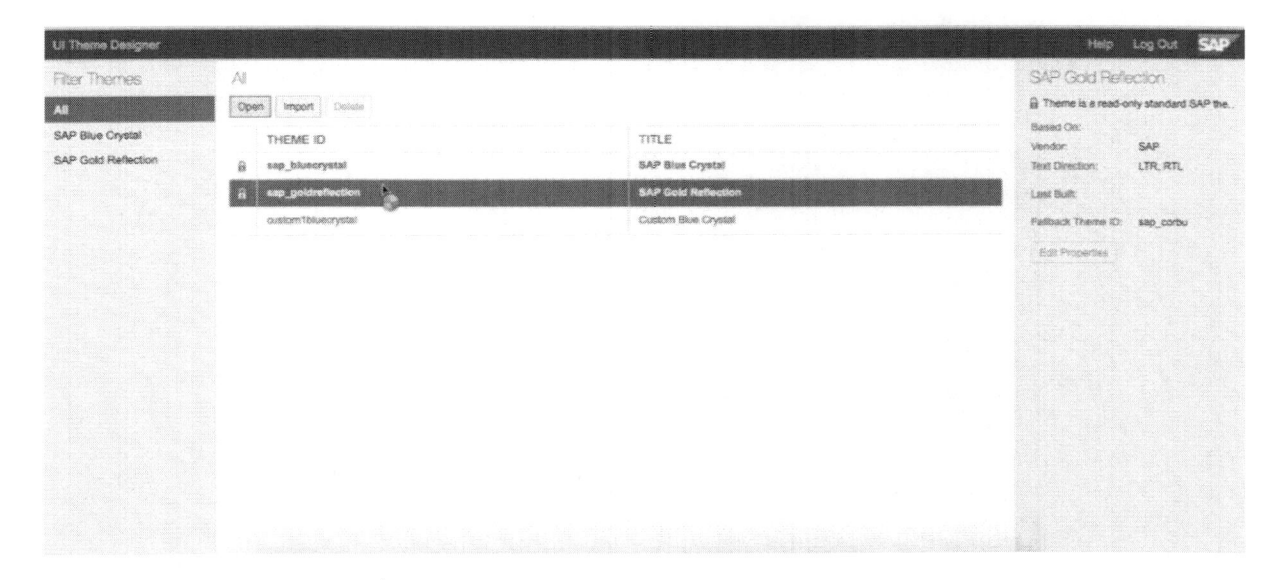

For now, we are going to use standard theme present in explorer for demonstration. Next option in the page you can see is SAP UI5 Application preview. Select that option and in the next page you can see two checkboxes *SAP Fiori launchpad* and *Explored*. We are going to select the Explorer. It will open the explorer application inside the theme designer.

Now here, we can quickly change the options like background color, brand color and highlight color. You can also create your custom CSS class and provide those values. There are color palette provided which can assist in making choices.

Learn SAP® UI5

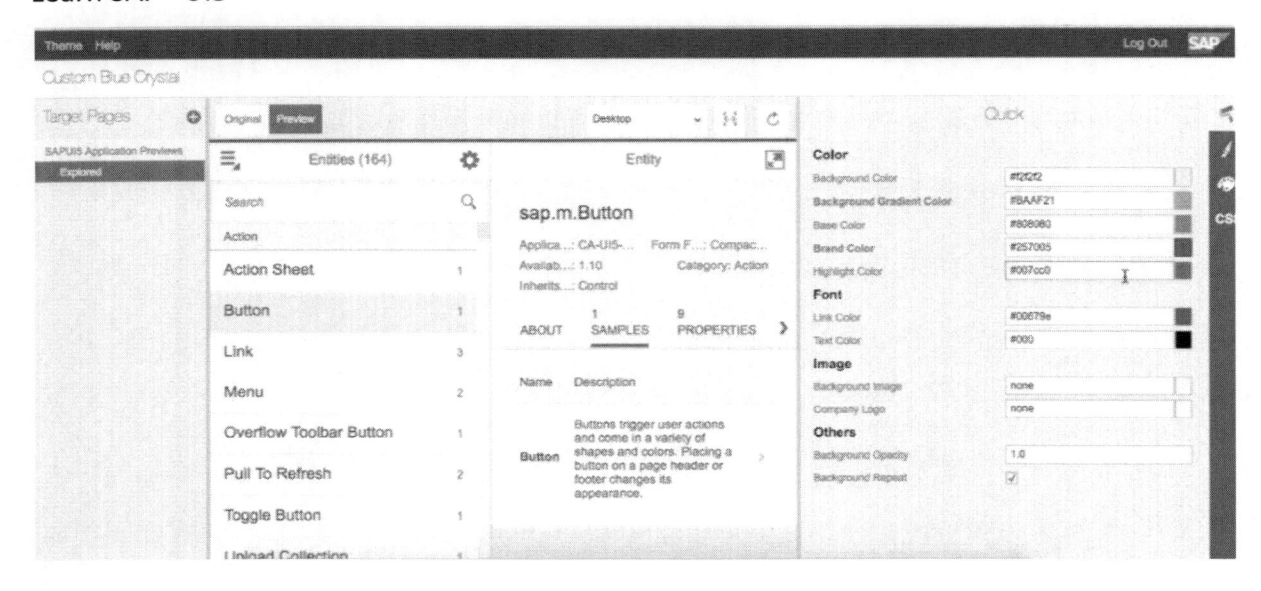

If you want to export the changes, you have to go to 'Theme' option present in top left and select 'Export'. You can also use the RTL (Right to Left) option if your app have to support RTL languages. It will show the export process and finally a zip file is automatically downloaded after completion.

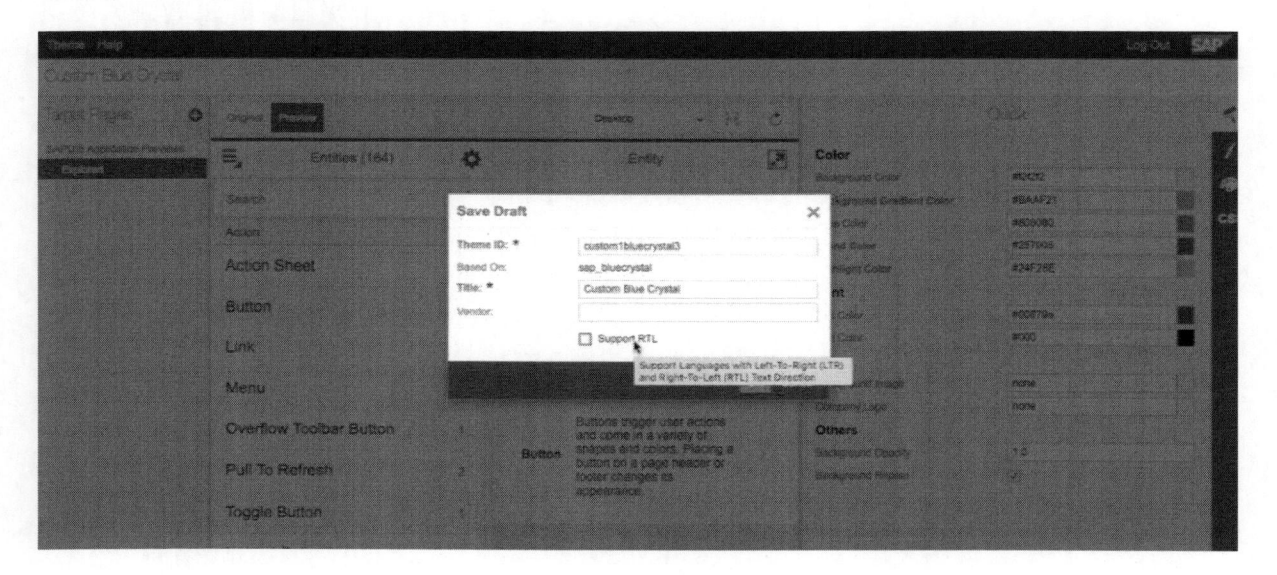

To use this new theme in eclipse. We have to follow below steps.

1. Find the location of the application in which we have apply the new theme.
2. Now go to the web content folders create a folder as resources.
3. Copy the 'Sap' folder present inside the UI5 folder and paste it inside the resource folder.
4. Change the theme name inside the index file.
5. Save and reload the page.

Learn SAP® UI5

One you reload the page you will be able to see the new theme applied to your application. In our case, we have applied the new theme to our 'Simple App' demo and it has changed the background, Input Box, and header style (as shown in below picture).

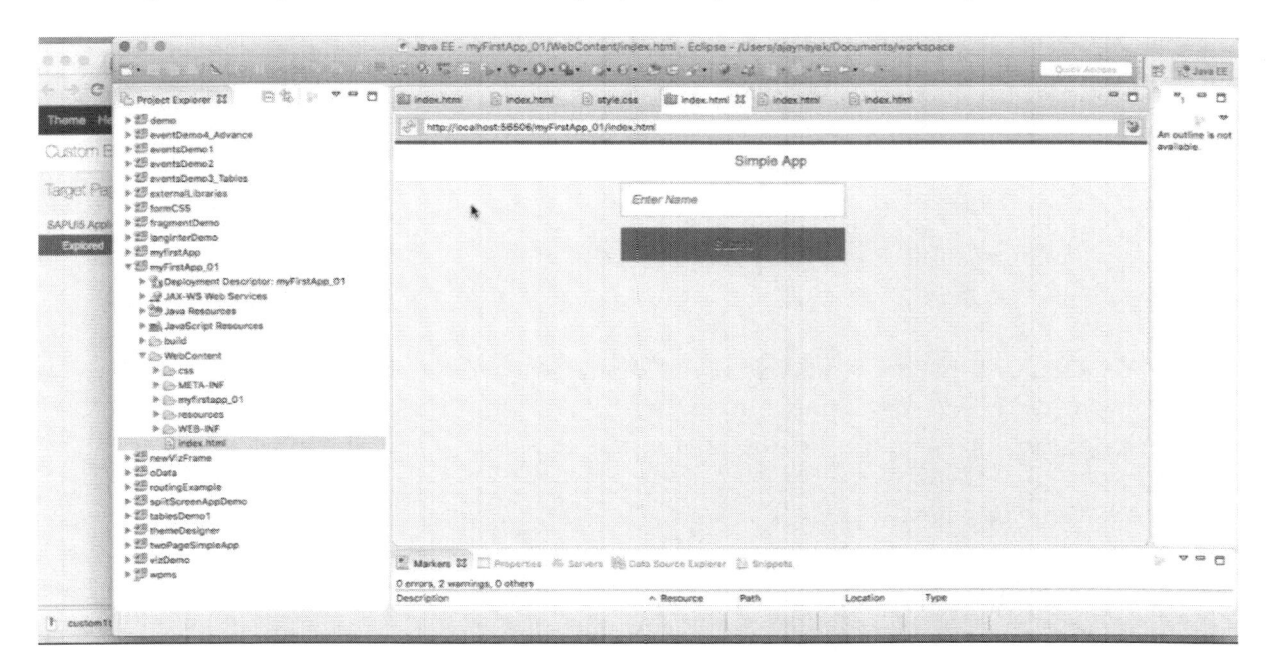

You can also check our SAPUI5 Professional Development video course for accelerated learning: here or use the below QR code.

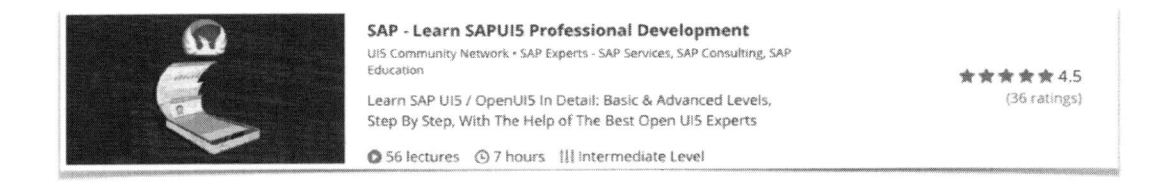

13. Using Events and Handling Events

EVENTS

Events are essential part of UI5 application. It tells how the application should respond, if certain user interaction happens. Some of the commonly known events are Click, Tap, Drag, Press etc. And some commonly used events are change, focus and key press etc.

For example in our simple input app example, we can have a 'change' event. And when user tries to write something or change an existing value then the action listener of this event is going to be fired.
The action listener function should ideally be implemented in controller and they should have a prefix 'on' before the name. This will help other developer to identify the action listener from rest of the available functions.

Now let us go to the API reference for the input box element and use the property for event listener 'liveChange'. If we go to view and add the 'liveChange' property:

```
var oSimpleInput = new sap.m.Input("idInput",{
        placeholder:"Enter Name",
            liveChange:[oController.onLiveChange,oController],
            //creating livechange function inside the controller

});
```

And in controller implement the action listener with name 'onLiveChange':

```
onLiveChange: function(oEvt){
    // degugger;
    var sValue = oEvt.getParameter('value');
        sap.m.MessageToast.show(sValue); //this toast function will
                        displays the text in nice toast format


},
```

And save and reload the application. The result is an input button, which will show a message toast at bottom of the screen, when you change any value in the input field:

Learn SAP® UI5

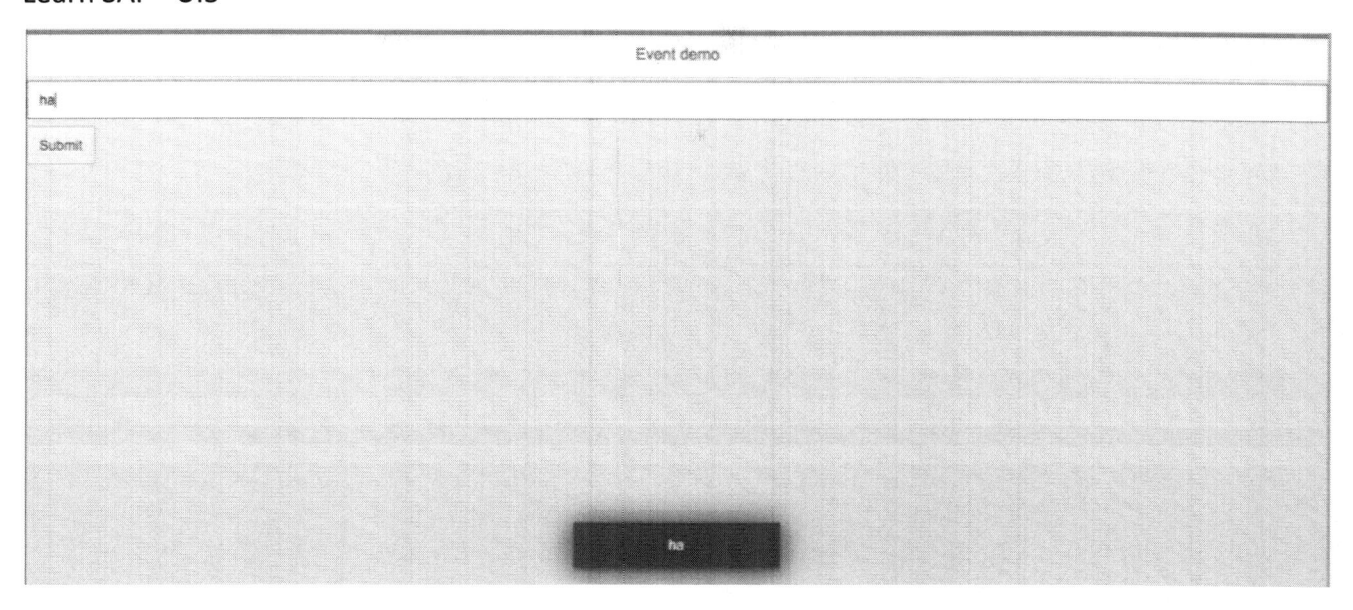

[Screenshot of Event demo page with input field containing "ha", Submit button, and a tooltip/button showing "ha"]

Events in Real Project

In real projects, use of events will be lot more complex. In this section, we will start increasing the complexity of the application. We already have a simple list in our application. In this application for now only list of animals are shown. If you click any items in that list, it will not go to the next page. Here we are going to add the navigation on item press.

Now create a new page in your application in eclipse and name it as second Page. Now add the second page inside the application using controllers Init function.

(Note: All the id's using inside your application should be unique or else it will show an error)

```
onInit: function() {

var page = sap.ui.view({id:"iddemo2",
viewName:"eventsdemo2.secondPage",
type:sap.ui.core.mvc.ViewType.JS});
app.addPage(page);
```

Now we have to add the event listener function. So go to the API reference and search for sap.m.List. Here in API reference we cannot find the event listener. So go to the super class of sap.m.List and look for the event listener property. Now use the property inside the view and then add the 'selectEventHandler' function inside the controller. Before going to add the function check that if the event is fired or not. Use a debugger keyword to verify it. Now we will find that when we use 'selectEventHandler' event will not fire and we will get error.

Learn SAP® UI5

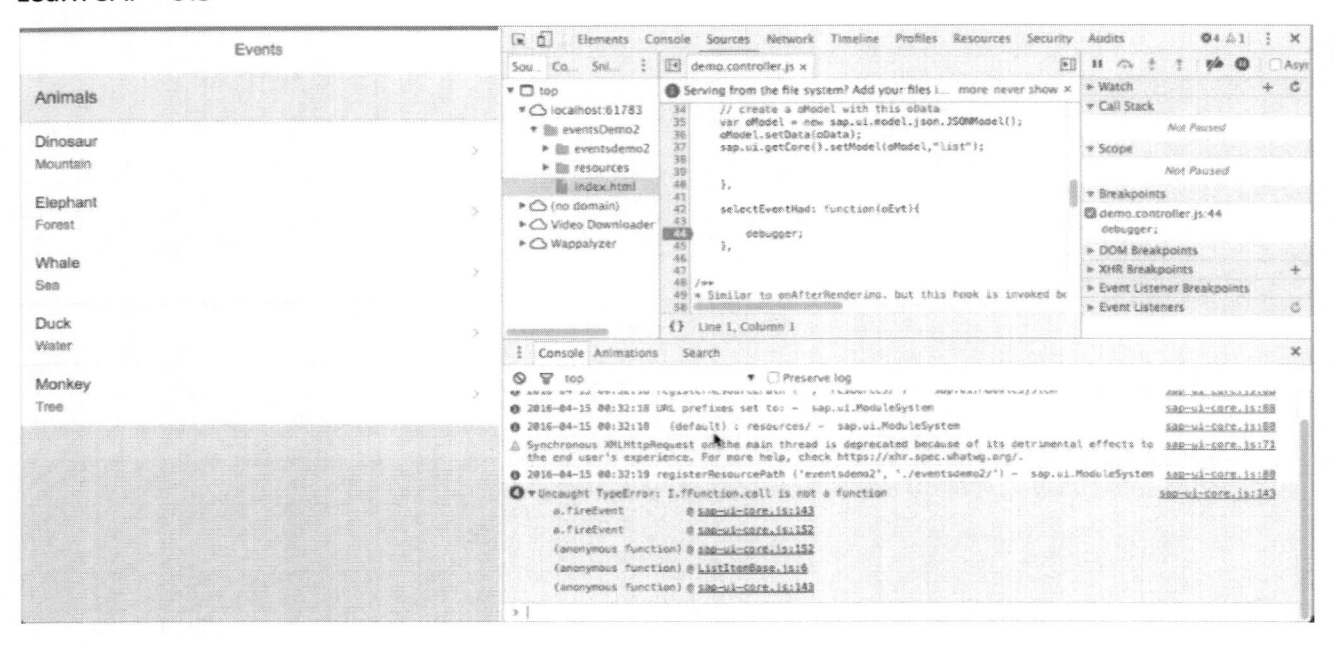

So let us go to the API reference and check the detail of select event property. Here we will come to know that the 'select' event is deprecated. It is important to verify the event usage and details before using it, if you are using it for first time. Now copy the 'selectChange' event instead of 'select'.

Below is the code for the View of the code:

```
createContent : function(oController) {


        // create a oList control
        var oList = new sap.m.List({
            headerText: "Animals",
            itemPress:[oController.onSelectEventHad,oController]
        });

        // bind the oList items to the oData collection
        oList.bindItems({
            path: "list>/names",
            template: new sap.m.StandardListItem({
                title: "{list>Name}",
                description: "{list>Place}",
                type: sap.m.ListType.Navigation

            }),

        });

        // create the oPage holding the oList
        var oPage = new sap.m.Page({
            title: "Events",
            content: [
                    oList
                    ]
        });
        return oPage;
```

}
});

When you are new to UI5 or working on some new components then you have to go through trial and error phase to reach to a working solution. If you have time in your hand then, it is better to experiment and reach the solution. Compare to finding the working piece of code from web because the iterative step of reaching to the solution will relieve a lot of more detail about usage and behavior of the element(s).

We can use console window to verify this operations. In this case, we verified that the oEvt.getParameters() will have the object 'listItem' and it is available then we use it in the controller. So now below is how the final controller event Handler function will look like:

```
onSelectEventHad: function(oEvt){

    var sVal =  oEvt.getParameters().listItem.getProperty("title");

    var oData = {           //Creating object for data
                "data" :sVal
    };
    sap.ui.getCore().setModel(new sap.ui.model.json.JSONModel(oData),"label");
    app.to("iddemo2");      //Binding takes place here

},
```

Inside the second page we have to also add a navigation button to come back to first page.

```
var oPage = new sap.m.Page({            //Creating oPage object for
                                                    second page
        title: "Second Page",
        showNavButton:true,     //To show Navigation button
        navButtonPress:function(){
            app.back();
        },
        content: [
                oLabel
        ]
});
return oPage;
```

Finally, we added the second page with navigation button. Now save the file and check if it is working. Below is the result of our application:

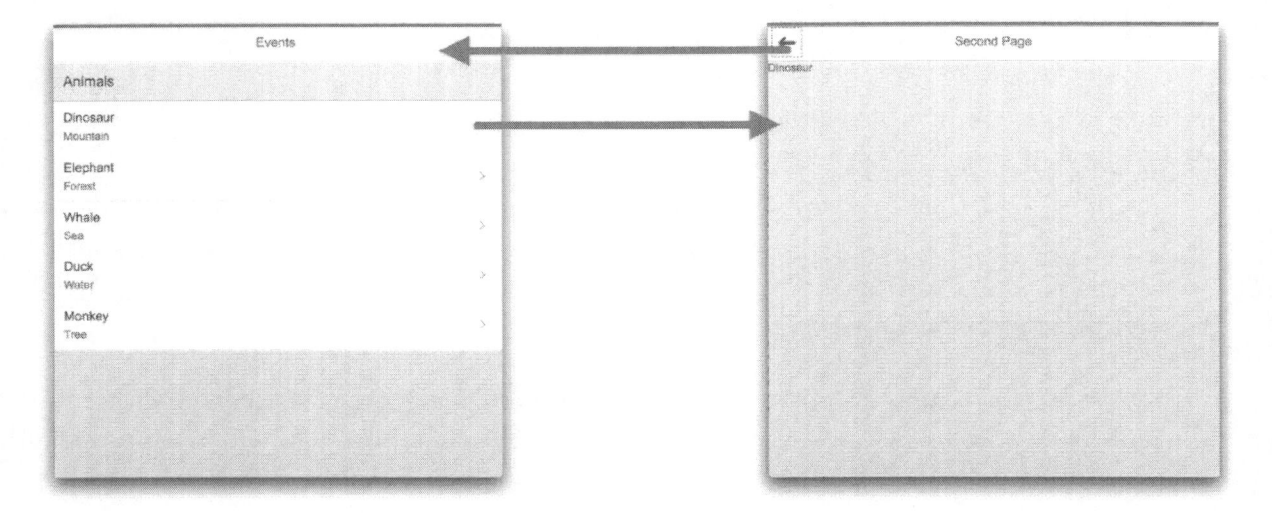

Events in Tables

In the previous example, we have seen the events in list. Now we use the same method and apply events for tables in this section. We already have the table example and in this example, we are going to add some functionality so if we click on some cell in the table it will go to next page and show the name and which row we clicked.

For that ,let's check the event property available in API reference and add the cell click event to the application. Let us go to eclipse and add the cell click event inside the view and pass the event handler function `goToNextPage`:

```
cellClick:[oController.goToNextPage,oController]
```

Now copy the name of the handler '`goToNextPage`' and create the function in controller

```
goToNextPage : function(oEvt){

debugger;
}
```

Now use the debugger to stop at the required debugging point, verify the parameters that the class accepts, and check if it gives the desired result. We will come up with:

```
oEvt.getParameters().rowBindingContext.getProperty("Name")
```

This gives the 'Name' property of the cell which we clicked on.

This is the final thing we will add in the controller:

```
goToNextPage : function(oEvt){   //Event function
```

```
            var sVal =
oEvt.getParameters().rowBindingContext.getProperty("Name");
            console.log(sVal);
              if(sVal !== undefined){        //Create the model only if the
                                                       value is available
                   sap.ui.getCore().setModel(new
sap.ui.model.json.JSONModel({
                       "data":sVal
                    }),"label") ;
              }
            app.to("iddemo2");      //This function allow to go second page
     },
```

Let us run the application and verify the result, also check if it goes to next page and comes back.

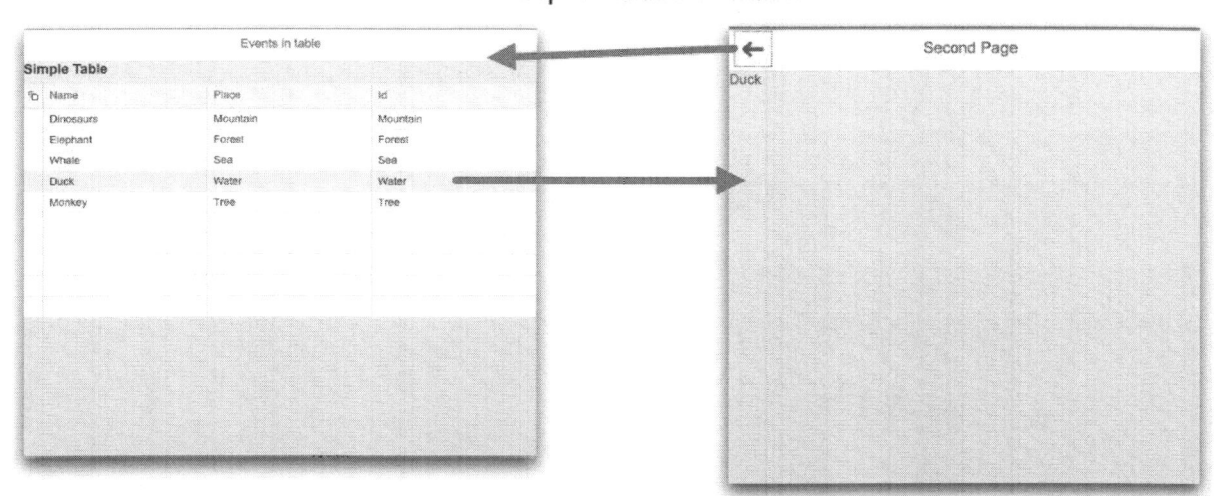

sap.ui.table.Table

Advance Events

Many a times you will get complex requirements. Sometimes specifically related to odd events. You may be asked to implement some of the events that are not present in the elements itself. One of the very popular examples is *drag*.

What we do when this situation arises?

Luckily, we have a huge number of libraries in Java Script world. One of the popular libraries is jQuery UI.

Now we have to create a button and make it draggable using UI5. For that, let us create a simple application with a button and add it in the page.

Now run the application. As you can see, the button is fixed and we drag it. We have to add a third party library here. Inside the index file, we need to add the jQuery UI libraries. The UI5 comes with a function `$.sap.require,` which allow us to add third party libraries:

Learn SAP® UI5

```
//Third party libraries (jQuery)
 $.sap.require('sap.ui.thirdparty.jqueryui.jquery-ui-core'); //Core library
$.sap.require('sap.ui.thirdparty.jqueryui.jquery-ui-widget'); //widget
library
$.sap.require('sap.ui.thirdparty.jqueryui.jquery-ui-mouse'); //mouse
library
      $.sap.require('sap.ui.thirdparty.jqueryui.jquery-ui-draggable');
                       //draggable library
```

The '$' denotes the jQuery Library. There are four libraries that are added to this application which are core, widget, mouse and draggable.

Inside the view, we need to add a special function called 'addEventDelegation' for adding for custom events:
    .addEventDelegation({
})

Add this inside createContent after the button function and inside this function add a function called onAfterRendering this will contain the draggable implementation:

```
createContent : function(oController) {

        varoBtn1 = new sap.m.Button({
              text:"Cool Button"
        }).addEventDelegate({     //For adding custom events

              onAfterRendering:function(oBtn){
                    $(oBtn.srcControl.getDomRef()).draggable({
                           cancel:true         //jQuery element with drag
                                               parameters using a DOM Reference
                    });
              }
        });

        var oPage = new sap.m.Page({
              title: "Event Advance",
              content: [
                    oBtn1
              ]
        });
    return oPage;

  }
```

Let's run the program and check, if you are able to drag the button present on the screen:

Learn SAP® UI5

Event Advance

[Cool Button]

In the next section, we will see the bubbling and capturing concept and how they define the event execution sequence.

Capturing and Bubbling

Capturing and bubbling are two ways in which an event can trigger. When you are working in a big project containing many events ,then sequence of execution of these events become important.

For example let's assume that we have a simple web app which with a DOM element tree. In the top level, we have a window with listener function cFW() for click events followed by a document with action listener function CFD(). And similarly HTML, Body and Button that all having its action listener cFH(), cFB() and cFBtn().

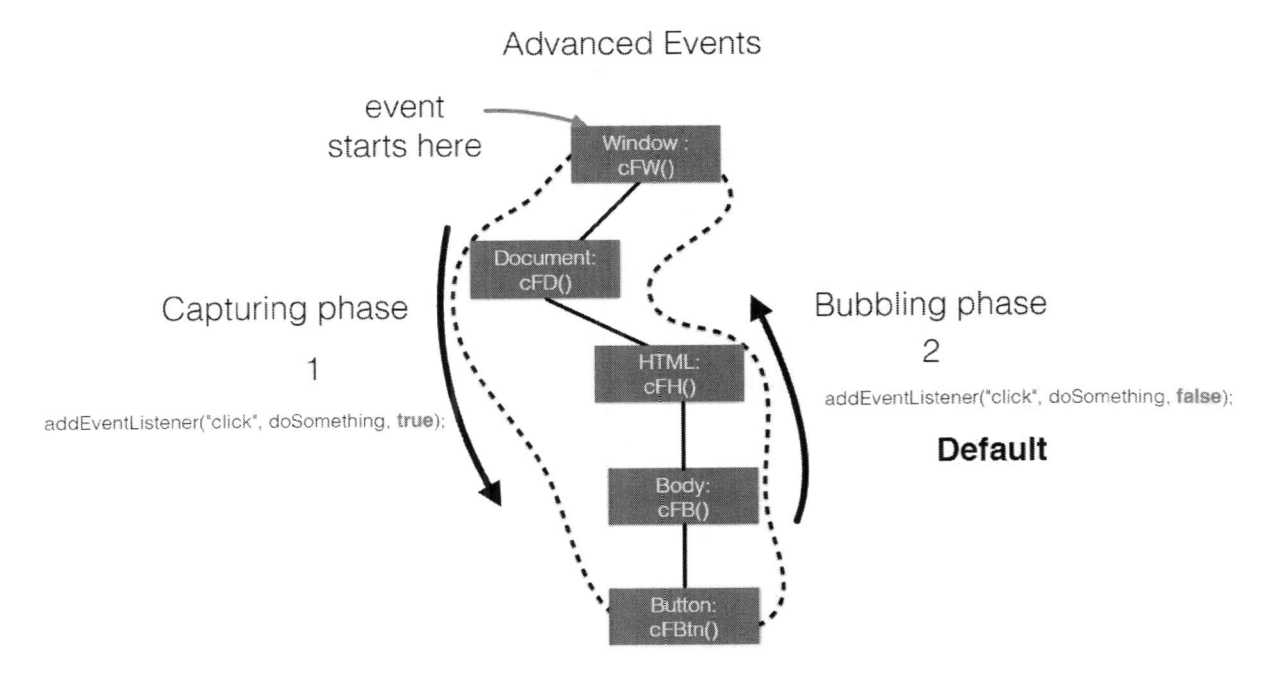

Advanced Events

event starts here → Window: cFW()
Document: cFD()
HTML: cFH()
Body: cFB()
Button: cFBtn()

Capturing phase
1
addEventListener("click", doSomething, **true**);

Bubbling phase
2
addEventListener("click", doSomething, **false**);
Default

Now if we click the button in the application. The control flow actually starts from the top it starts from the cFW(), cFD(), cFH(), cFB() and finally cFBtn(). When the control flow reaches to the button two things can happen before it goes back to top level again. It will execute

Learn SAP® UI5

our cFBtn() function while the way down or while the way up. You may think here what the difference is.

Capturing: The control flow travelling from up to down is called capturing phase. We can use capturing if we pass the third argument for event listener function as true*addEventListener("click", doSomething, true)* .

Bubbling: The control flow travelling from down to up is called Bubbling phase. We can use bubbling if we pass the third argument for event listener function as *false addEventListener("click", doSomething, false)*.

In this case, each of the intermediate functions gets the control flow twice. If they have the event handler for that function then it will be executed twice.

To explain the difference, we can take the example of our draggable button. Now if add a click event listener to this button and its immediate parent element in DOM tree. And in first case we:

- Execute the event handler of button in Bubbling phase(passing false in 3rd parameter)

    document.getElementById("_button0").addEventListener("click", function(){
        console.log("btn")
            }, false);   //Mentioned false so it will be executed in bubbling phase

- Execute the event handler of its parent element also in Bubbling phase(passing false in 3rd parameter)

    document.getElementById("_page0-cont").addEventListener("click", function(){
        console.log("sect")
            }, false);   //Mentioned false so it will be executed
                                                                       in bubbling phase

Now if you click on the button then it will show below result in console:

Learn SAP® UI5

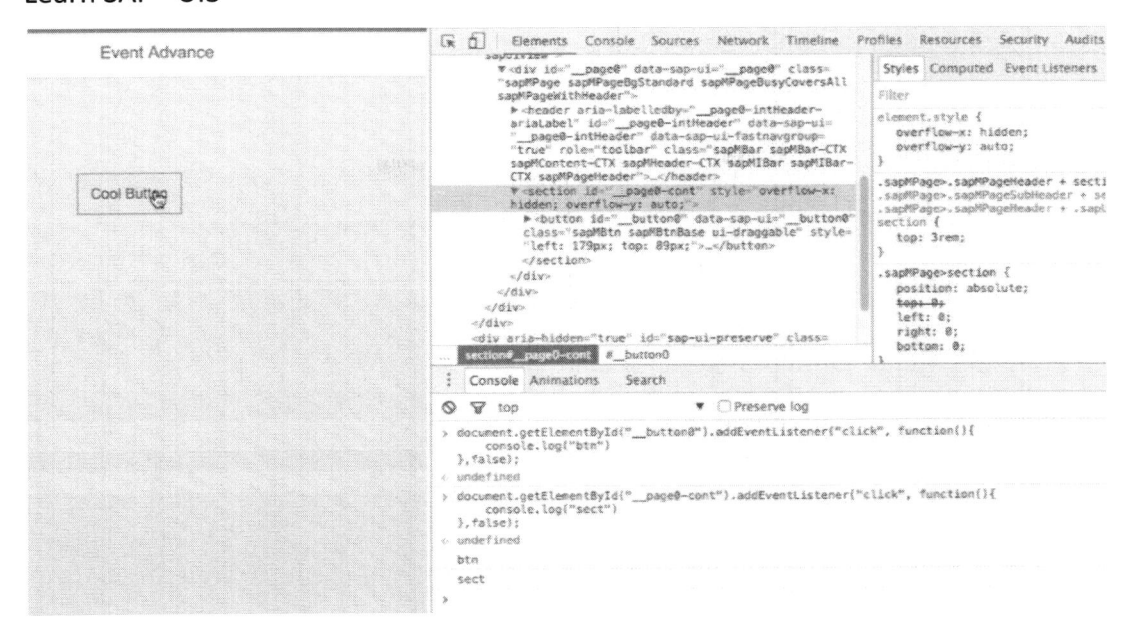

Now if we change parent element execution sequence by making it execute in capturing phase (by passing true in 3rd parameter):

document.getElementById("_page0-cont").addEventListener("click", function(){
    console.log("sect")
            }, true);   //Mentioned false so it will be executed
                                                              in capturing phase

Now the sequence of result will be reversed in console.

This was a simple example is to understand the difference and impact of capturing and bubbling events.

Note: Some of the browsers like Internet Explorer do not support event capturing. Therefore you need to use event bubbling there.

You can also check our SAPUI5 Professional Development video course for accelerated learning: here or use the below QR code.

81

Learn SAP® UI5

SAP - Learn SAPUI5 Professional Development
UI5 Community Network • SAP Experts - SAP Services, SAP Consulting, SAP Education

Learn SAP UI5 / OpenUI5 In Detail: Basic & Advanced Levels, Step By Step, With The Help of The Best Open UI5 Experts

★★★★★ 4.5
(36 ratings)

56 lectures • 7 hours • Intermediate Level

Learn SAP® UI5

14. Miscellaneous Controls in UI5

UX3 Control – SHELL

Sometimes you want to develop an application and you don't have much time to rethink about the user experience details. And also if your users are going to use the application mostly in desktop environment. Then in that case going for Shell based application is a good idea. Shell comes with lot of the out of box properties and functions, which makes the development quite easy and fast. To use Shell you have to use the *sap.ui.ux3.Shell*control.

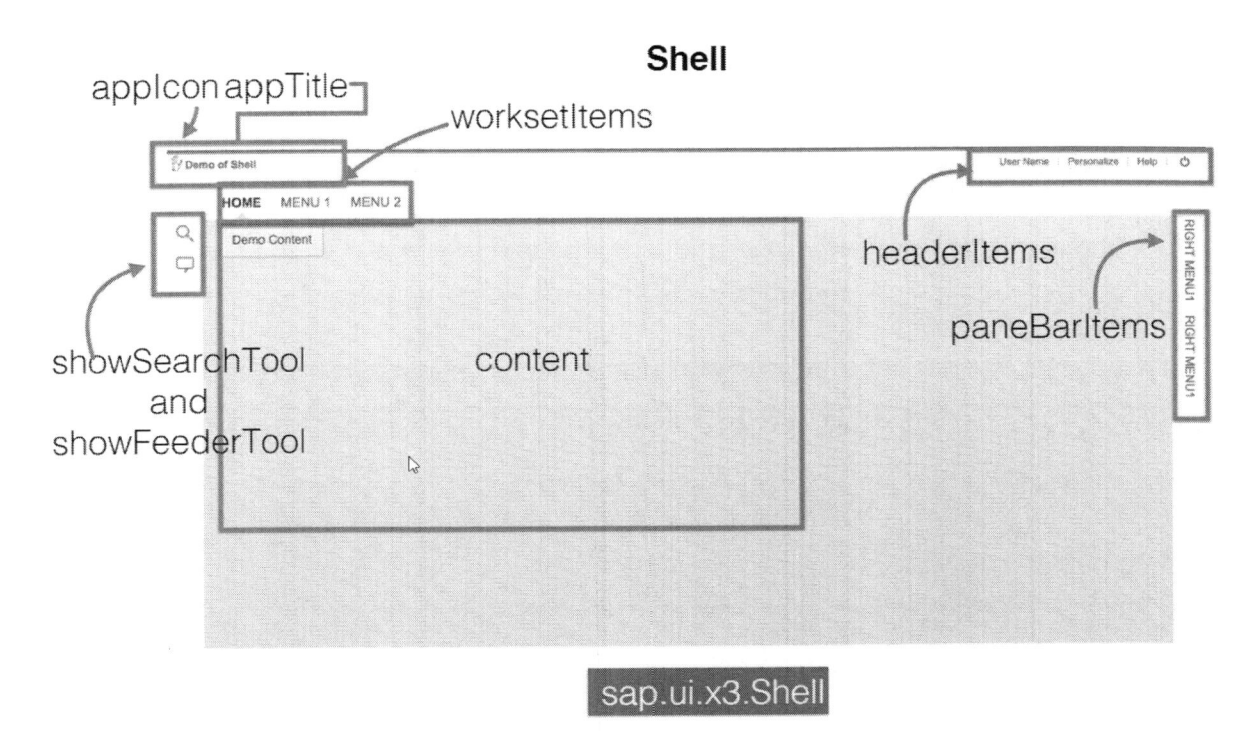

Shell

appIcon appTitle
worksetItems
showSearchTool and showFeederTool
content
headerItems
paneBarItems

sap.ui.x3.Shell

Let's create a simple shell app, as shown in above picture where we have a home tab and two menu items. You can place any content inside the menu tab like table, list, combination of table and list etc. For now let's keep it simple and place a button there.
In the left hand side, we have a search box and a feeder toolbox. Also there is a header which provides options to add login or log out feature. In the right side, we have sliding menu. We can also place list, table and more.

So to start the development, we go to the API reference to search about the Shell using the 'sap.ui.ux3.shell' keyword. Where you can get a lot of details and also simple example of its implementation.
Now create a new project in eclipse and as we are going to use Shell based controls so we are adding libraries 'sap.m, sap.ui.ux3' in bootstrap code.

Learn SAP® UI5

Below is the UI5 code which will result in the Shell based on our simple requirement:

```
<script>
    jQuery.sap.require("sap.m.MessageBox");

    var oShell = new sap.ui.ux3.Shell({

        appTitle : "Demo",
        showLogoutButton : true,
        logoutButtonTooltip : "Logout",
        showSearchTool : true,
        showInspectorTool : true,
        showFeederTool : true,
        showTools : true,
        showPane : true,

        }.placeAt("content");
```

Now add the other properties to the shell.

```
        worksetItems : [ new sap.ui.ux3.NavigationItem({ //navigation panel
            text : "Home",
            key : "Home",           //Key for home button
            press : function(oEvt) {
                sap.m.MessageToast.show("Home pressed!");    //This
                    will show a message toast when home button is pressed
            }
        }), new sap.ui.ux3.NavigationItem({
            text : "Menu 1",
            key : "M_1",
            press : function(oEvt) {
                sap.m.MessageToast.show("Menu1 pressed!");    //This
                    will show a message toast when menu1 button is pressed
            }
        }) ],
        content : [ new sap.m.Button({
            text : "Simple Button"
        }) ],
        worksetItemSelected : function(oEvt) {

            sap.m.MessageToast.show(oEvt.getParameter("id"));

        },
        paneBarItems : [   //Pane bar items

        new sap.ui.core.Item({
            text : "Demo Item"
        }) ]

    }).placeAt("content");
```

Learn SAP® UI5

Fragments

Fragments are like actionable pop ups which comes handy in mobile screens or tablet screens. Specifically, when you require action from the user it will block the background and the user can only see the popup contains some list items or some input forms.

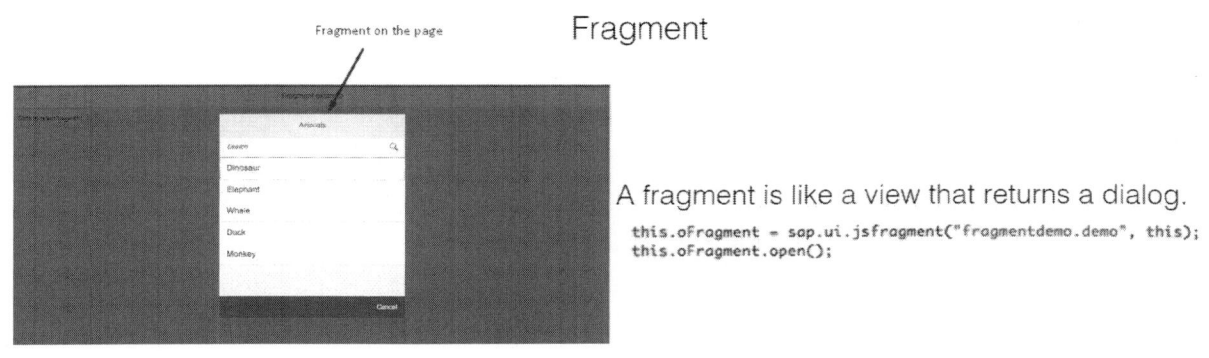

Fragment

A fragment is like a view that returns a dialog.

```
this.oFragment = sap.ui.jsfragment("fragmentdemo.demo", this);
this.oFragment.open();
```

new sap.m.SelectDialog

It shares the controller with the view.

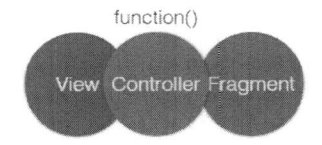

One interesting thing about fragment is, it shares the same controller with the view. For example if the user want to search in the list then those event handler is to be written on the same controller.

So let us create a simple project. Where we will have a button and when we press the button, then the fragment should appears. Below is the code, which we will add in the view for placing the button in the page.

```
createContent : function(oController) {

    var oButton =  new sap.m.Button({    //Creating button object

        text:"Click to open fragment",
        press:[oController.openFragment,oController]
    });

    var oPage = new sap.m.Page({   //Creating page
        title: "Fragment example",
        content: [
            oButton
        ]
    });
    return oPage;
```

85

Learn SAP® UI5

```
    }
  });
```

Now we need to create a JavaScript file inside our webcontent with same name as view controller 'demo.fragment.js'. And add the `jsfragment` code as below:

```javascript
sap.ui.jsfragment("fragmentdemo.demo", {

    createContent: function(oController) {

var oItemTemplate = new sap.m.StandardListItem({
        title: "{list>Name}",
        active: true
    })

    var oSelDialog = new sap.m.SelectDialog({
        noDataText: "Empty",
        title: "Animals",
         liveChange: [oController.handleSearch, oController],//Used for
                                        search option in the fragment
        confirm: [oController.handleConfirm, oController],
        type: "Active"
    });

        oSelDialog.bindAggregation("items", "list>/names", oItemTemplate);
                                                        //Binding the Data

return oSelDialog;
    }
});
```

Now in controller we will, open the fragment when the button is pressed.

```javascript
        openFragment : function(oEvt){

            if(this.oFragment === undefined){

                this.oFragment = sap.ui.jsfragment("fragmentdemo.demo",
this);
                this.oFragment.open();

            }else{
                    this.oFragment.open();
            }
```

And now, if we save and run the application we will get below result:

Learn SAP® UI5

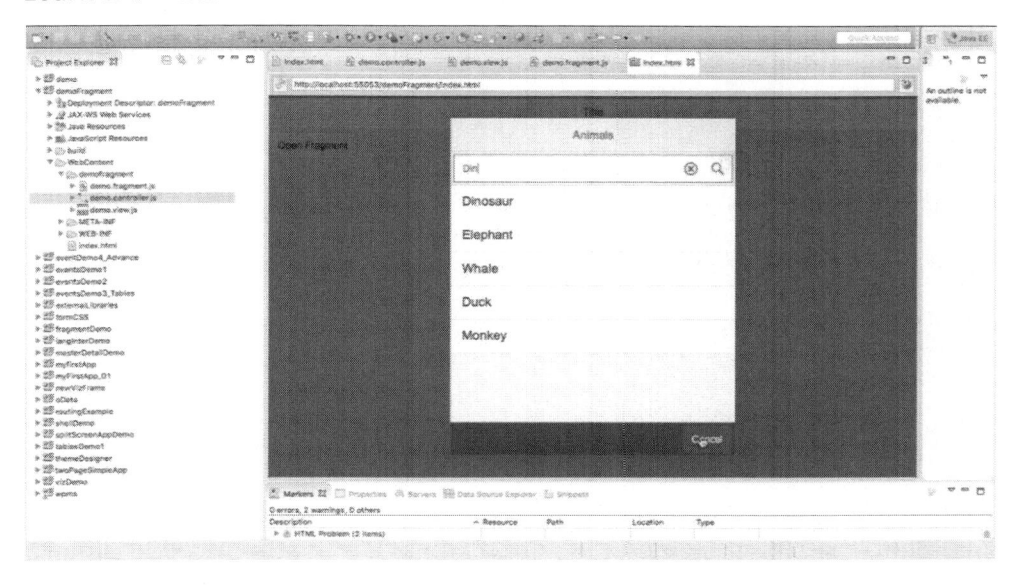

Split Screen Application

A split screen application contains a master page and a detail page. The master page contains the content and when you click on the content, you will get the detail of the particular content. The real advantage of using the split screen application is adaptable to smaller devices.

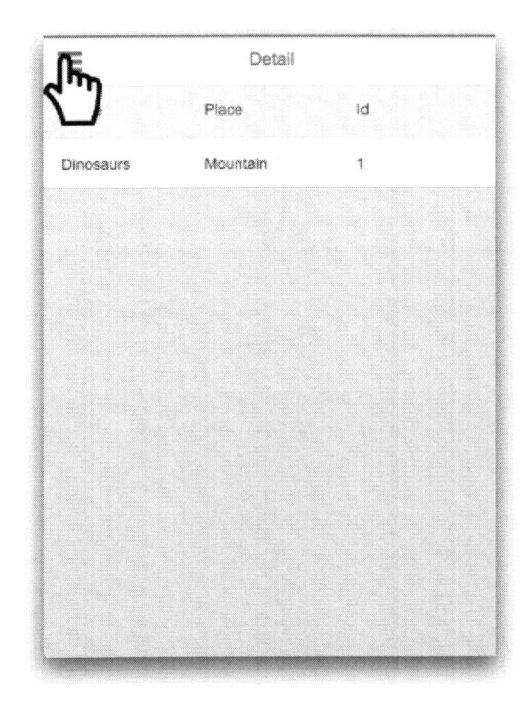

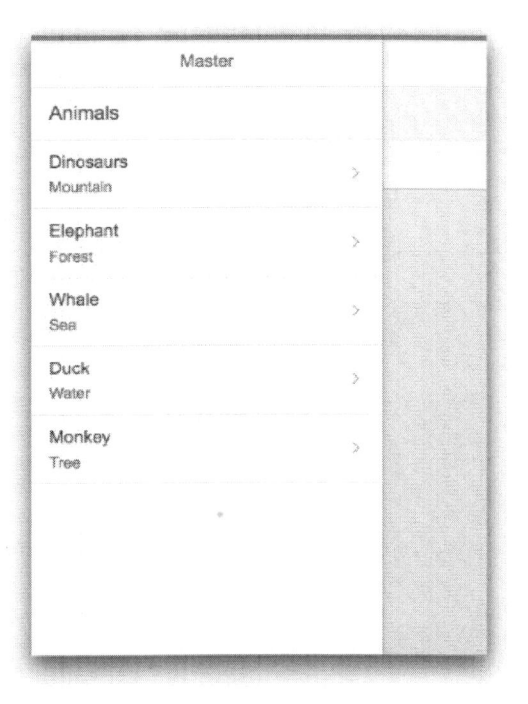

Detail Page

Master Page

87

Learn SAP® UI5

Let us create a simple split screen application in eclipse. We already have a list example with event navigation. In this case, Master page will contain the list items. The second page will contain the details of the item which will be selected in a Table. So we can reuse the content of table example and place in the detail screen.

The main new change will come in the index page. Here we are going to remove 'sap.m.App' because we are going to use 'sap.m.SplitApp'. And add the mode as: `sap.m.SplitAppMode.ShowHideMode`.

Below is the code to be placed in Index page:

```
<script>
        sap.ui.localResources("masterdetaildemo");
        var app = new sap.m.SplitApp("idSplitApp",{
                mode:sap.m.SplitAppMode.ShowHideMode //Show
                                            or hiding property
        })
        var masterPage = sap.ui.view({id:"idmaster1",
viewName:"masterdetaildemo.master", type:sap.ui.core.mvc.ViewType.JS});
        app.addMasterPage(masterPage); //Master Page

        var detailPage = sap.ui.view({id:"idDet2",
viewName:"masterdetaildemo.detail", type:sap.ui.core.mvc.ViewType.JS});
        app.addDetailPage(detailPage);   //Detail page

        app.placeAt("content");
</script>
```

Here we added the master screen and detail screen to our application. Once you create the master and detail page and place list and table respectively, then on running the applicationyou will see below result:

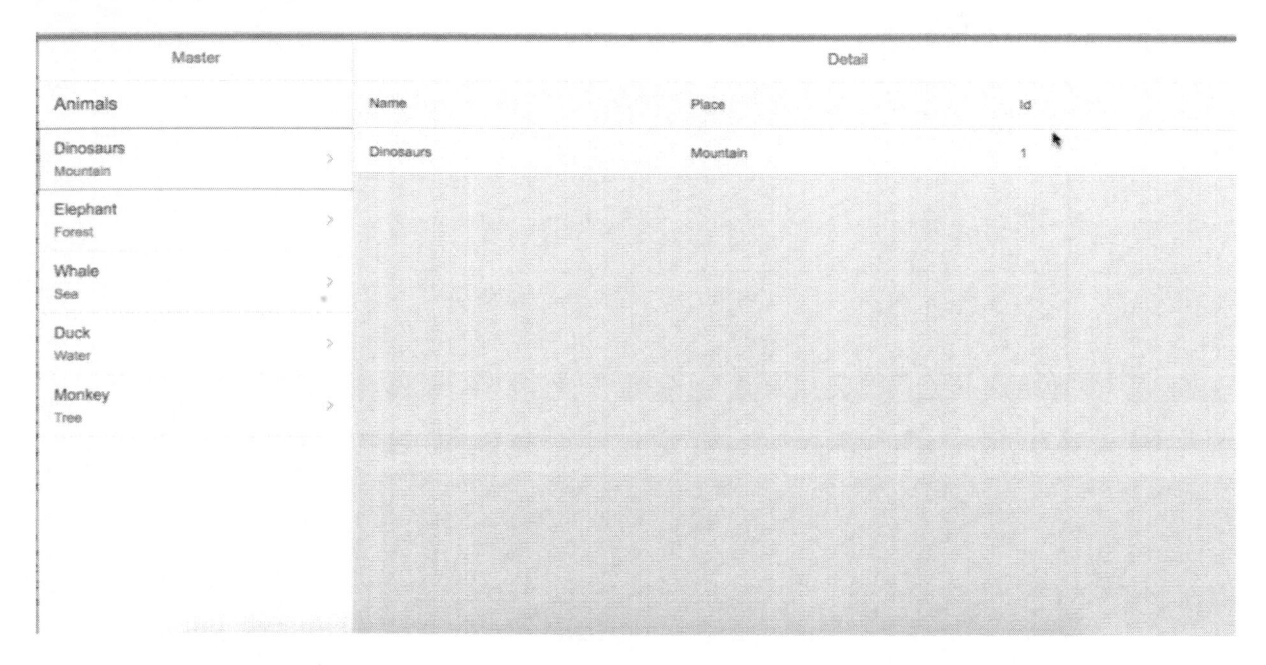

Master		Detail		
Animals		Name	Place	Id
Dinosaurs Mountain	>	Dinosaurs	Mountain	1
Elephant Forest	>			
Whale Sea	>			
Duck Water	>			
Monkey Tree	>			

Learn SAP® UI5

You can also check our SAPUI5 Professional Development video course for accelerated learning: here or use the below QR code.

15. App Improvement Elements

FORMATTER

Formatter provides more control in the way data is represented once it is bound to certain element. For example, if we have to create a list that contains name of animals and the locations they belong to concatenated together in the title. In this case, we have to put it together in a single property.

One real example is the date. Date can be represented in many different formats like dd/mm/yy or mm/dd/yy etc.(dd is day, mm is month and yy is year)

Let us look at the first example where we can append 'Name' and 'Place' of the animals together:

Without Formatter the data binding will look like :

```
oList.bindItems({
        path: "/names",
        template: new sap.m.StandardListItem({
            title: "{Name}",//Key with curly braces
            description: "{Place}"//Key with curly braces
        })
});
```

With Formatter the data binding will look like :

```
oList.bindItems({
        path: "/names",
        template: new sap.m.StandardListItem({
            title: ({
                parts: [{
                path:"Name",     //Key with path without curly
                                                             braces
                type: new sap.ui.model.type.String()
                }, {
                path:"Place",
                type: new sap.ui.model.type.String()
                }],
                formatter: function(sName, sPlace){
                //all parameters are strings
                return sName +" : "+sPlace; // Concatenation
                }
        })
        })
});
```

The differences between these two are:
- In first case, we are passing key directly inside curly braces.
- And in the second case we have a `formatter` function which returns what will be the content of the binding.

Learn SAP® UI5

Below will be the result of the code with and without formatter:

Internationalization and Localization

Internationalization and Localization allows our app to be more accessible for international audience with their regional languages. Most of the countries are not native English speakers. You may work on some project that involves customers from non-English speaking countries. English might be the second and third languages in some countries. In these cases you need to customize your application into their preferred language.

Assume that user of your application are from USA, Germany and China. And in this case you have to make the app compatible with three languages depending upon from which region it is accessed.

To translate the app in compatible languages we have to add the i18n properties. For US customer it will be English, for German customers it will be in German and the Chinese customers it will be Mandarin. The first step will be to check the local language using function:

```
sap.ui.getCore().getConfiguration().getLanguage()
```

This will give you the local language of your application. Once you get the local language then link the appropriate language file to an app. For that, we have to create a model called i18n and bind it in our code. The i18n model will be loaded from different files where each file will be specific to one language.

Below you can see the content of the view, where we will have i18n named model:

```
createContent : function(oController) {
    var oBtn = new sap.m.Button({
        text:"{i18n>greet}"  // Button name with local language
    })

    var oPage =  new sap.m.Page({
        title: "i18n Example",
        content: [
                oBtn
        ]
    });
    return oPage;
}
```

Now create a folder called 'i18n' and create the three files inside the folder and name it as i18.properties, i18n_de.properties and i18n_ch.properties. Inside that file we have to write the property greet with the different languages in appropriate files. Eg. in English 'greet=Hello', in German 'greet=Halo' and for Mandarin we will use the Google translate use the text insidei18_ch file. In eclipse once you enter mandarin language, it will automatically translates it into Unicode characters.

Inside the demo controller, add code which identifies which file type to open depending upon location:

```
onInit: function() {

        var sLoc = sap.ui.getCore().getConfiguration().getLanguage();
        var i18nPath = "i18n/i18n";
        if(sLoc === "de_DE"){   //German language region code
            i18nPath = i18nPath +"_de.properties";
        }elseif(sLoc === "zh-Hans"){   //Chinese language region code
            i18nPath = i18nPath +"_ch.properties";
        }else{

            i18nPath = i18nPath +".properties";
        }

        var oi18nModel = new sap.ui.model.resource.ResourceModel({
            bundleUrl:i18nPath //Creating model
        });
        sap.ui.getCore().setModel(oi18nModel,"i18n");
    },
```
Note:To get all the regional language codes you can go to Below URL :

https://wpcentral.io/internationalization/

Now if we run the application and want to see, how the application will look if user from China opens the app. Then for that we can add language suffix to our URL '?sap-ui-language' with the language value.

Learn SAP® UI5

Example: localhost:55913/i18nDemo/index.html? ?sap-ui-language=zh-Hans

This will display the button in Mandarin language:

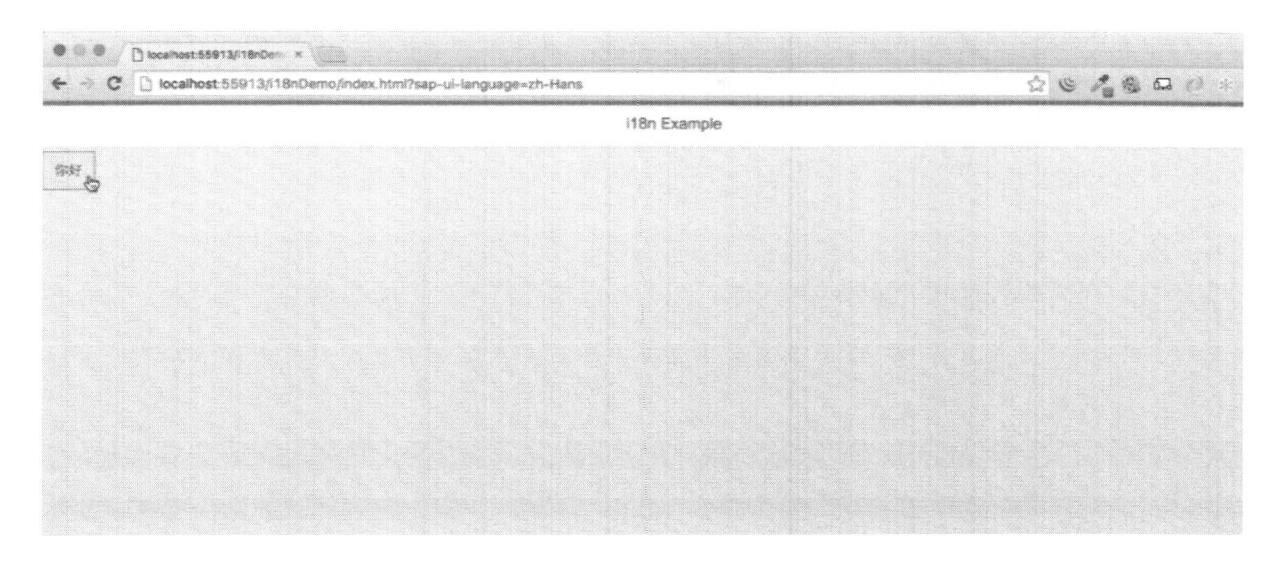

You can also check our SAPUI5 Professional Development video coursefor accelerated learning: here or use the below QR code.

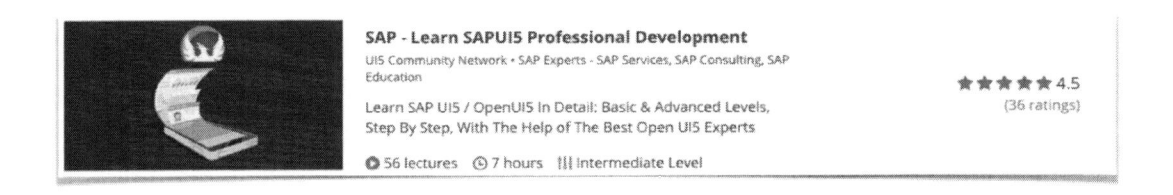

16. Data Visualization Using UI5

Viz : Bar Chart

Now we are going to see how to use visualizations capabilities ofUI5. For this purpose, we will be using Viz library, which are only present in SAPUI5 and not present in Open UI5. And from versions 1.34 of SAPUI5,there has been a big change on the way we should use it. So let's see how to make use of these libraries.

To create a simple bar chart with Viz, we have to create
- Flattened dataset
- Axis.

Flattened dataset

Flattened dataset is an object that defines the binding. It has two main parts. First one is called dimensions and second one is called measures. Dimensions tell us what we are comparing and measure will tell us the value, which we are comparing.

Axis

Axis also has two main parts that are dimensions and measure. Dimensions tell us what we are comparing. Measure will tell us the value, which you are comparing.

Once you created the axis and flattened dataset then you need to define the VizFrame.

```
var oVizFrame = new sap.viz.ui5.controls.VizFrame();
```

We need to provide three important details to this VizFrame:
1. Flattened dataset
2. Type of chart (Bar or Pie Chart)
3. Axis

Learn SAP® UI5

Bar Chart

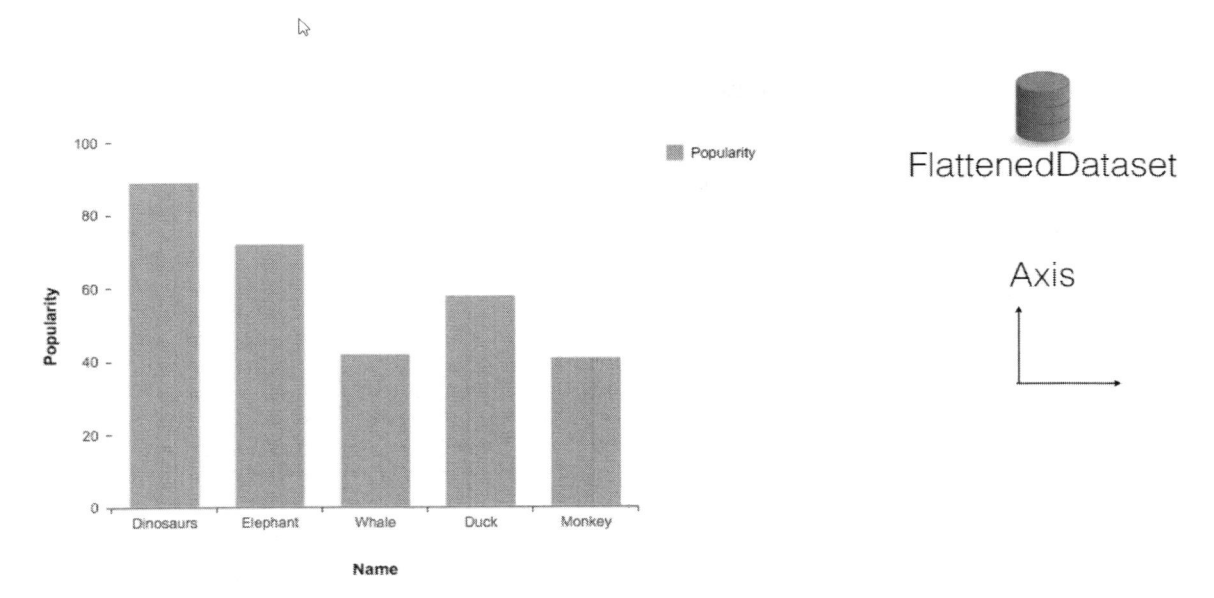

Also in index.html we have to include the additional *sap.viz* library:

```
<script src="resources/sap-ui-core.js"
        id="sap-ui-bootstrap"
        data-sap-ui-libs="sap.m,sap.viz"//viz library
        data-sap-ui-theme="sap_bluecrystal">
</script>

<script>
        sap.ui.localResources("newvizframe");
        var app = new sap.m.App({initialPage:"iddemo1"});
        var page = sap.ui.view({id:"iddemo1",
        viewName:"newvizframe.demo",
        type:sap.ui.core.mvc.ViewType.JS});
        app.addPage(page);
        app.placeAt("content");
</script>
```

Inside the demo view we have to add the flattened dataset (data is going to be our old animal list here).

```
createContent : function(oController) {
    varoVizFrame = new sap.viz.ui5.controls.VizFrame();

    //Create Vizdataset to feed to the data to the graph
    var oDataset = new sap.viz.ui5.data.FlattenedDataset({ //Flattened dataset
        dimensions : [{   //dimensions
            name : 'Name', //Pass the name of animals
            value : "{pie>Name}"
        }],

        measures : [{    //Measures
            name : 'Popularity',
            value : '{pie>Popularity}'
        }],
```

Learn SAP® UI5

```
            data : {
                path : "pie>/names"
            }
        });
        var feedValueAxis = new sap.viz.ui5.controls.common.feeds.FeedItem({
                                                                //Value axis
'uid': "valueAxis",
'type': "Measure",
'values': ["Popularity"]
        });
var  feedCategoryAxis = new    //Category axis
sap.viz.ui5.controls.common.feeds.FeedItem({
'uid': "categoryAxis",
'type': "Dimension",
'values': ["Name"]
        });

        oVizFrame.addFeed(feedValueAxis); //adding dataset to value axis
        oVizFrame.addFeed(feedCategoryAxis);
        oVizFrame.setVizType('bar');
oVizFrame.setDataset(oDataset);
```

On running above application we will be able to see simple bar chart in our result:

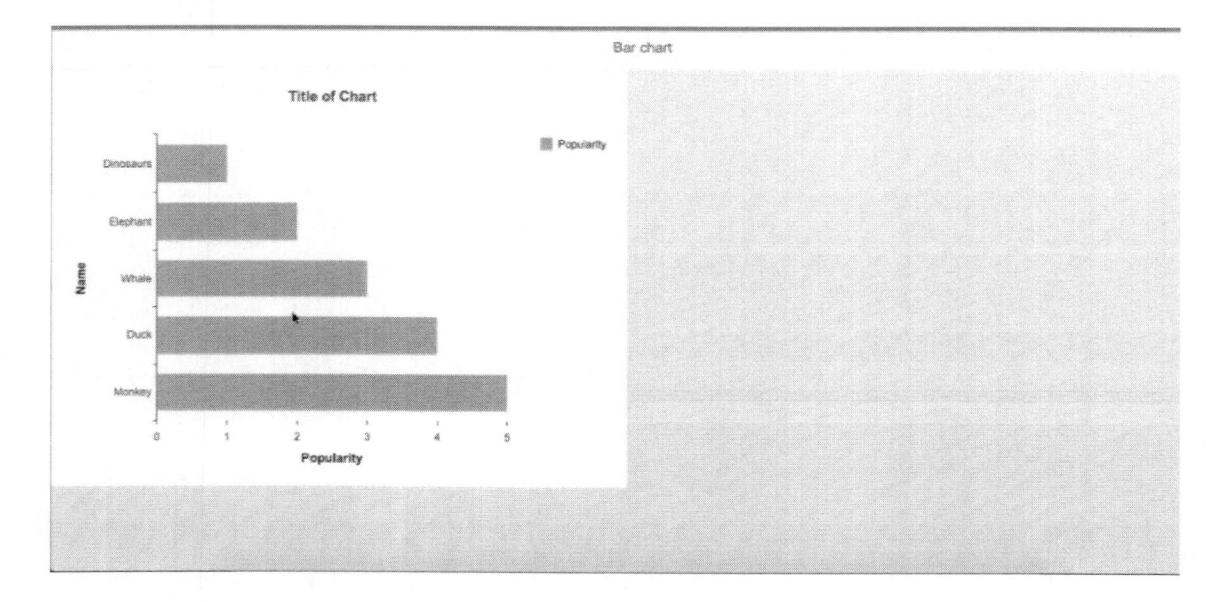

Viz : Pie Chart

Process of creating Pie chart is similar to the Bar chart. So let's create a simple application using pie chart with our animal list. We have to create a Flattened dataset and axis. The data binding is going to be same as it was in case of bar chart and also the dimensions and measures as well.

So we as well we need three important parts to be defined:
1. Flattened dataset
2. Type of chart (Bar or Pie Chart)
3. Axis

Learn SAP® UI5

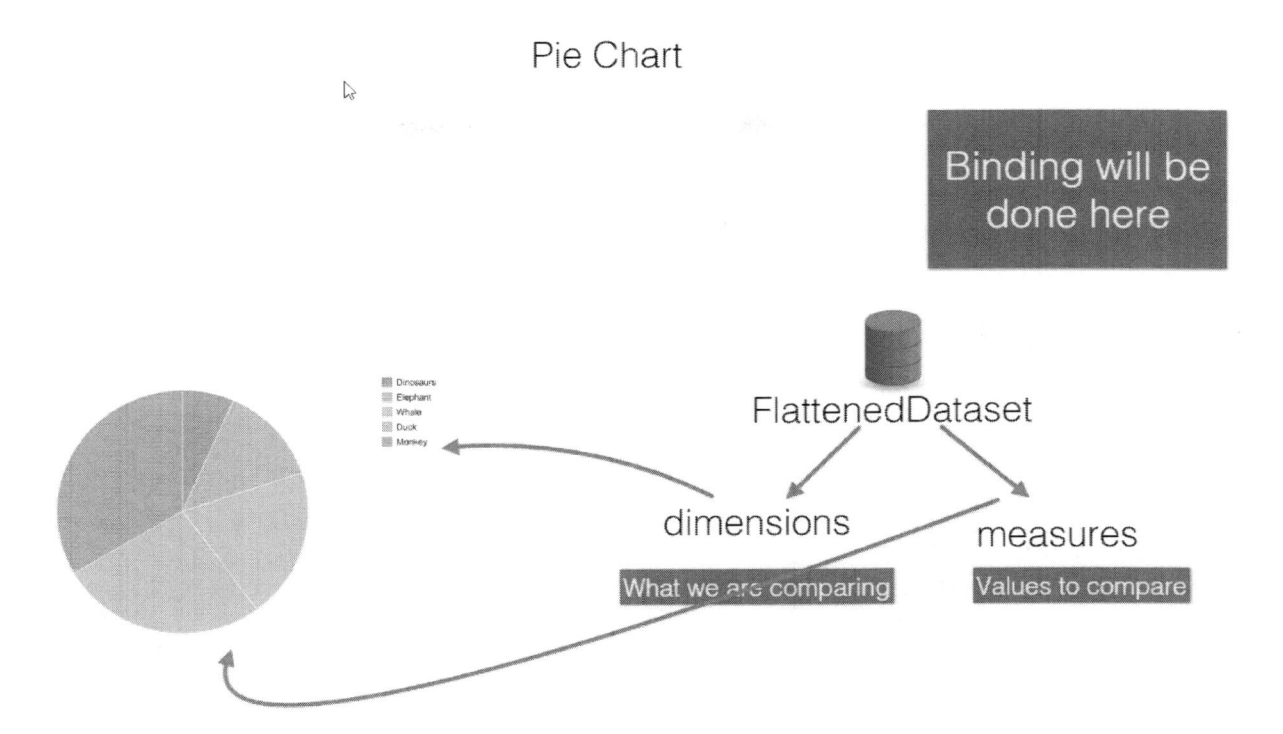

Pie Chart

In case of Pie chart Axis will represent colors which differentiate different `Dimension`.

```
var feedValueAxis = new sap.viz.ui5.controls.common.feeds.FeedItem({
//Value axis
'uid': "size",
'type': "Measure",
'values': ["Popularity"]
        });
var  feedCategoryAxis = new //Category axis
sap.viz.ui5.controls.common.feeds.FeedItem({
'uid': "color",
'type': "Dimension",
'values': ["Name"]
            });
oVizFrame.addFeed(feedValueAxis); //adding dataset to value axis
      oVizFrame.addFeed(feedCategoryAxis);
      oVizFrame.setVizType('pie'); //Changed to pie
          oVizFrame.setDataset(oDataset);
      })
```

You can see the API reference for detail implementation, but for now the above changes will be just fine to render a simple Pie chart. Save and run the app and you will get anoutput, which looks like:

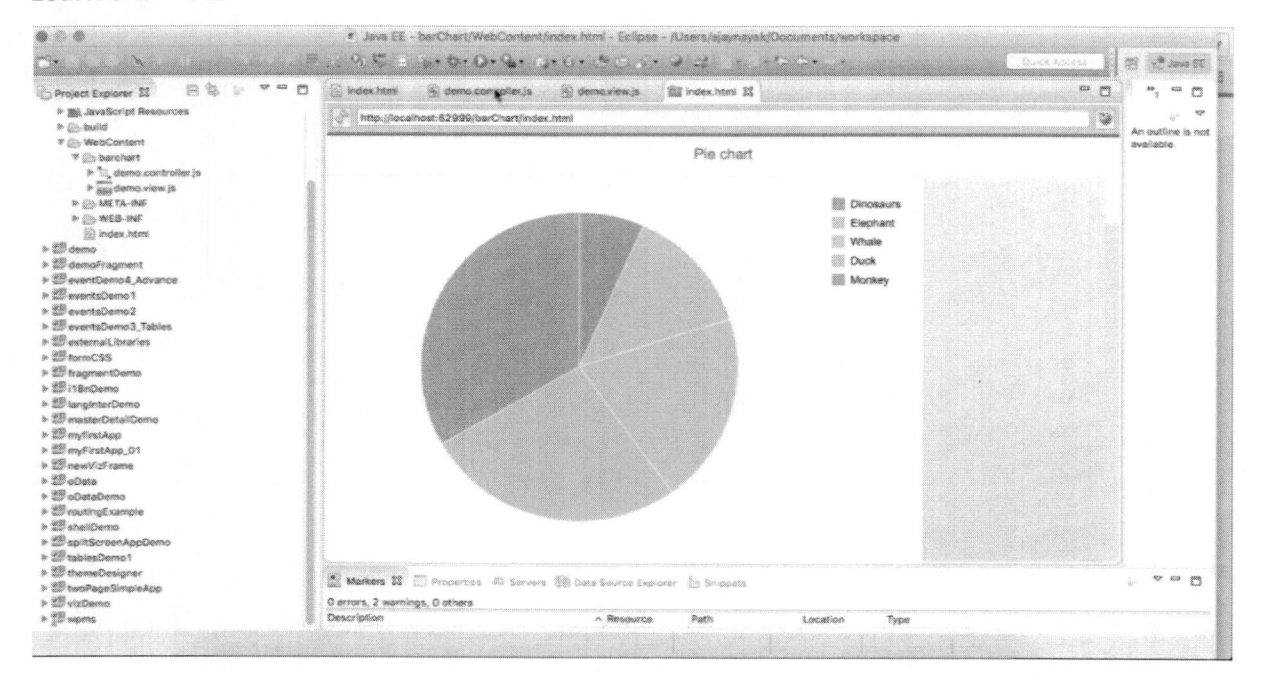

Learn SAP® UI5

KPI Tiles

KPI tiles are one of the most essential parts of visualization in Fiori based applications. KPI stands for Key Performance Indicator. In this section, we are going to see how to create KPI Tiles and add it to the KPI tile container.

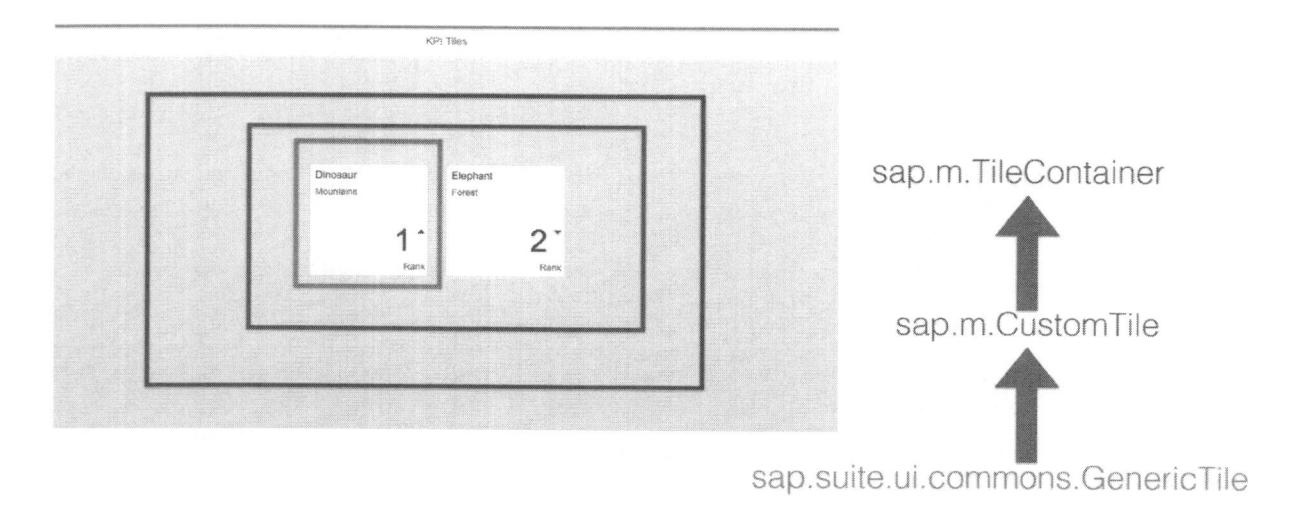

Steps to create KPI Tiles:
- Create a generic tiles
- Place the generic tile inside the custom tile
- Put all the custom tile inside the tile container

We also need to add the 'sap.suite.ui.commons,sap.ui.core,sap.viz' libraries in the index page in addition to 'sap.m'

Learn SAP® UI5

```
<script id='sap-ui-bootstrap' type='text/javascript'
src='https://sapui5.hana.ondemand.com/resources/sap-ui-core.js' data-sap-ui-
theme='sap_bluecrystal' data-sap-ui-
libs='sap.m,sap.suite.ui.commons,sap.ui.core,sap.viz'></script>
<!-- load the mobile lib "sap.m", the layout lib and the "sap_bluecrystal" theme -
->


<script type="text/javascript">
var oDinoT = new sap.suite.ui.commons.GenericTile({    //Creating tile for dinosaur
header: "Dinosaur",
          subheader: "Mountains",
          tileContent: [
new sap.suite.ui.commons.TileContent({
                    footer: "Rank",
                    content: [
new sap.suite.ui.commons.NumericContent({
                                                //Contains numeric content
indicator: "Up",
                              value: "1",
                              valueColor: "Good"
})
               ]
          })
     ]

     });
var oEleT = new sap.suite.ui.commons.GenericTile({
                              //Creating second tile for Elephant
header: "Elephant",
          subheader: "Forest",
          tileContent: [
new sap.suite.ui.commons.TileContent({
                    footer: "Rank",
                    content: [
new sap.suite.ui.commons.NumericContent({
                              indicator: "Down",
                              value: "2",
                              valueColor: "Good"
})
               ]
          })
     ]

     });
</script>
```

Now if we run the code, it will result something like:

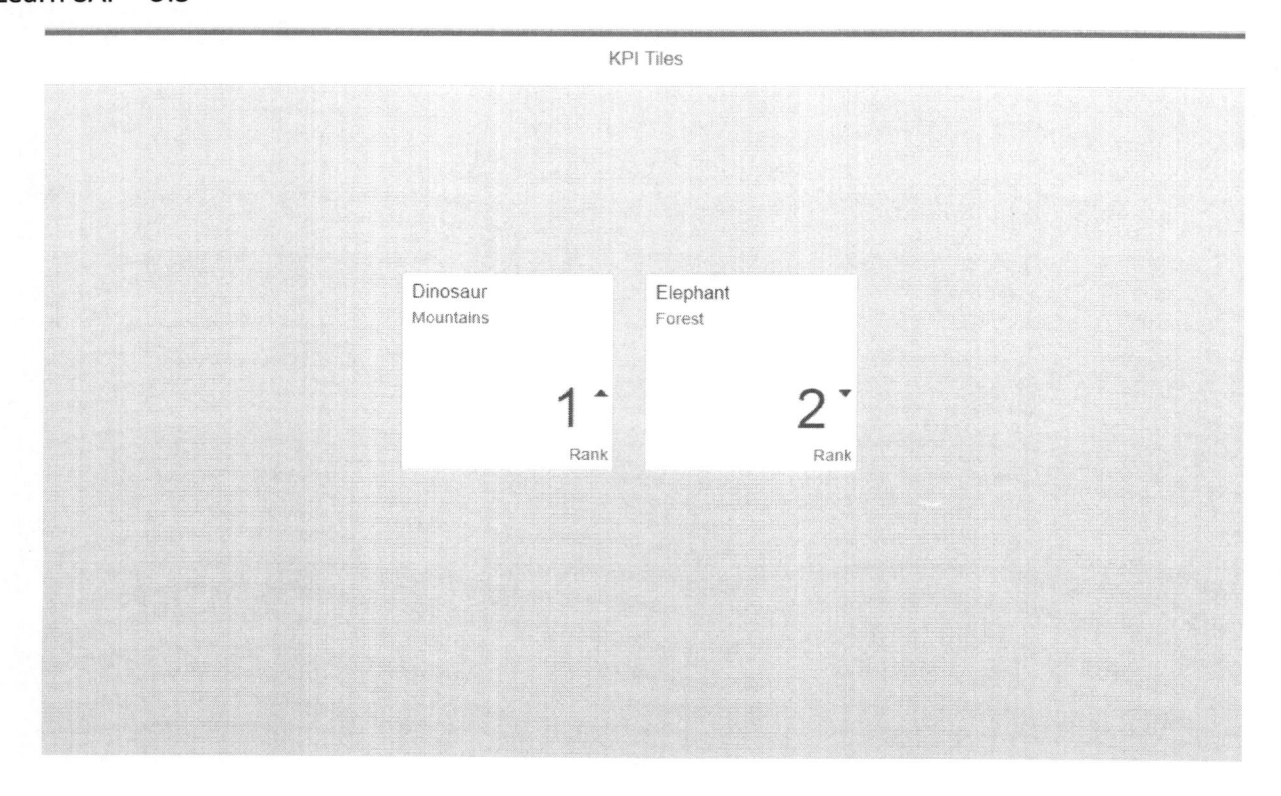

Learn SAP® UI5

KPI Tiles

Dinosaur	Elephant
Mountains	Forest
1 ▲	2 ▼
Rank	Rank

You can also check our SAPUI5 Professional Development video coursefor accelerated learning: here or use the below QR code.

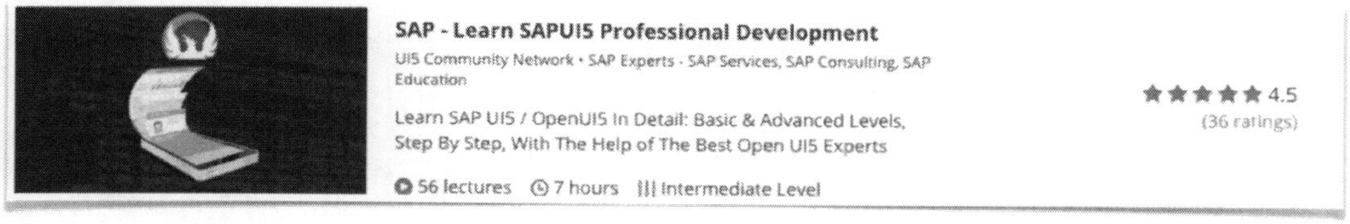

Learn SAP® UI5

Referencing and Bibliography

- Open UI5 API Reference : https://openui5.hana.ondemand.com/
- UI5CN official blog : http://ui5cn.com/
- Udemy UI5 video course : https://www.udemy.com/learn-sapui5/
- Open UI5 Explored : https://openui5.hana.ondemand.com/explored.html

Printed in Great Britain
by Amazon